A Christian's Guide to Speaking Secular

From The Spiritual Puzzle Project Series

by Bob Bernet

Edited by: Pat Leedy

Cover Illustration by: Gary Sanders

Website Design by: Kaiser Design Studio

Printed in the United States of America

First Printing 2023

ISBN 979-8-218257-56-9

What is the Spiritual Puzzle Project?

When I first began thinking about spirituality and Christianity, I was trying to understand different spiritual worldviews and how they all fit together. After studying many spiritual and philosophical subjects from many different angles, I felt like I was trying to put a puzzle together, but I did not have the picture on the puzzle box. My goal with the Spiritual Puzzle Project is to help people see the big picture on the puzzle box of spirituality so they can decide for themselves where their piece fits in the Spiritual Puzzle.

The better you understand the world around you and its origins and our spiritual nature, the better you can deal with all the difficulties of everyday physical life.

The Spiritual Puzzle Project does not claim to have all the answers, but it will give you plenty of topics to think about to help you develop your unique spiritual, Intellectual, and physical gifts.

How to Read this Book

This book is not meant to entertain you. The goal of this book is to help you think deeper and harder about Christianity than you normally would. It also has many suggestions about how to understand and explain Christianity in secular language.

If you are a deep-thinking Christian and you want to understand the spiritual basics of Christianity in a way you have not heard before, this book should help. The introduction and the first two chapters describe the psychological development of spiritual understanding. Most people are not used to combining psychology and spirituality. Starting with chapter three, the information is more history based than psychology based, so those chapters are easier to understand the first time through.

It may help to read this book twice. Consider reading small sections at a time and stopping to think about what you have read before moving on. And for those parts you don't initially understand, you might want to power through those the first time and revisit them later. To paraphrase an old quote, "The more you put into this book, the more you will get out of it."

The book tries to explain deep subjects like the Image of God and the Holy Spirit, which can be a little difficult the first time through. These are concepts that add great depth to your understanding of Christianity. Do not be hesitant to take time and pray about these subjects as you read.

Acknowledgements

This book and the Spiritual Puzzle Project are a product of inspiration, love, and support from many people who made an indelible impact on my life. I dedicate the Spiritual Puzzle Project Series books to Dorothy Leedy and the Leedy Family. Thank you, Dorothy, for all you and your family did to help bring my wife halfway around the world to the USA, which allowed her to become the beautiful, loving and amazing lady she is today. I would not be the well-rounded person I am today without all the love and generosity you gave to her.

To Pat Leedy, thank you for all you have done to edit and help me develop the ideas in this book. You were my sole encourager, coach, and editor for the first two years as the Spiritual Puzzle Project came into existence.

Thank you to my wife Pasna, who was the first person to get me to travel outside my comfort zone outside the USA, to see other parts of the world which helped me understand how different and diverse the world really is. You helped me realize that the best way to grow and learn more about yourself is to talk to someone who is very different and has different ideas than you do. We can only grow by comparing what we know to what we do not know.

I continue to dedicate my books to my deceased parents Bob and Trudy who made sure I received a good education and taught me about the joy you receive when you step outside your comfort zone, and you give of yourself to help others.

Recent authors and speakers I have followed and been influenced by as I developed the ideas in this book are:
Jordan Peterson, Bishop Robert Barron, Michael Guillen, David Limbaugh, Peter Marshall, Dr. Peter Kreft, James Emery White.

Many Thank You's go to:

Hodge Drake, Paul Jones, and especially my kids and Daughters in laws, Ashley and Jyotsna. You all have been my constant encouragers. You have listened patiently while I verbalize the many random thoughts about spirituality that go through my head on a regular basis.

Bob Faul and John Thompson, for being extra sets of editing eyes and the first to fight your way through the original draft.

David Braughler of Braughler Books, who has been helpful with all the publishing and editing challenges over the years.

Jeff Eberlein of, brandit FOR GOOD, and Barbara Reaman of Marketing Services Inc., you both have provided encouragement as well as helpful advertising and marketing advice throughout the process.

Gary Sanders who has been patient and diligent throughout the artwork process. Ed Sawicki of Cincinnati, Ohio, for "over and above" photography services.

All Biblical references are from the New International Version unless noted.

Giving Back
A portion of the proceeds of this book will be donated to help create generational change for vulnerable, abused, and forgotten children in Cincinnati, Ohio; Kerala, India; and Africa.

For more information on helping children, please check out: Greaterproject.org.

Contents

The Psychological Foundation of Spirituality

Chapter 1   Spiritual Consciousness Development   9

Chapter 2   Three Stages of Individual and   21
Social Development

The History of Spiritual Development

Chapter 3   Ancient Gods, Abraham, and Moses   27

Chapter 4   The Image of God   37

Chapter 5   Jesus, The first Human Rights Advocate   43

Chapter 6   Spiritual Consciousness Revolution,   55
The Holy Spirit and The New Covenant

Chapter 7   The Rise of the Church   69

Chapter 8   Understanding America's Roots   75

Chapter 9   A Step Backward, Darwinism and   81
Existentialism

Chapter 10   What is Your Worldview?   93

Chapter 11   Politics and Spirituality   101

Chapter 12   The Way Forward: Spiritual Life and   107
Spiritual Death

Questions and Answers   115

Introduction

To help someone learn a second language the teacher must have command of both languages. If you want to understand or help someone else learn math, you don't start with algebra, you start with the basics. The Bible is the most amazing piece of literature and history ever put together. Whether or not you consider yourself a Christian, the life lessons you can learn from reading the Bible are as helpful, and probably more thorough than anything else you will find. The good news of the Gospel and the life of Jesus and His teachings are very deep, and there are many levels of meaning. When we try to teach these concepts to others, we need to be able to explain it starting with simple language that they can understand. A big problem with trying to help non-Christians learn about Christianity is that many Christians struggle with knowing how to express the true depth and beauty of the Christian message. Most people are not comfortable sharing the good news for many different reasons.

The first goal of this book is to help Christians and non-Christians understand the remarkable and beautiful spiritually uplifting message of Christianity. The second goal is to help Christians learn how to explain the good news in familiar language that is comfortable for non-Christians to understand. If you are a non-Christian and you want to understand the spiritual basics of Christianity in a way you have not heard before, this book should help. This book is not intended to be a scholarly work. It is intended to be an easy-to-understand description of Christianity with suggestions on how to help non-Christians understand the beauty in common, non-religious, and non-threatening language.

This book will explain why I translate the good news of the gospel into secular language by calling it: **The history of the spiritual consciousness development of the human race.**

The Bible tells a story that is very deep and complex in some ways, but very simple in other ways. Part of the story is about God helping humanity realize what I call ***The Great Paradox of Human Existence***.

Humans are *spiritual in nature*; we are spirits that live in a body. This concept can be a hard thing to grasp. Since humans come to consciousness in a physical body it can be hard to understand our spiritual nature. Because we start in a physical body, many people get caught up in the physical world and never realize the full impact of what it means that humans have a spiritual nature. Physical laws and spiritual laws are very different. As children, we are taught many physical or scientific laws of the physical world, but most people are never taught that there is also a spiritual dimension to the world and that there are spiritual laws that are very different from the physical laws. To be a fully developed human, you must understand both the physical and the spiritual laws, which are very different and can seem contradictory, but once you understand them you see how everything fits together.

Another topic that will be discussed is that before science advanced and super computers were invented, it was very easy to see a picture of an ape and a picture of a man and think that it is easy to get from a few atoms floating in space, to an ape, to a human. In those days, science pointed away from a spiritual dimension to reality. In the last few decades, super-computers and advanced science and physics computer models are indicating it is impossible to get from a few proteins floating in space to the great complexity of the human body and the universe by chance. Later in the book, we will discuss the evolving relationship of science to spirituality.

Speaking Secular

I believe one of the best ways to start teaching non-Christians about Christianity is to refer to Christian principles as "Spiritual Principles." I also like to use the phrase *Understanding Spiritual Literacy* as a first step toward understanding Christianity. If people first agree there is some sort of spiritual dimension to reality, then I believe we can make the case that Christianity is the spiritual worldview that makes the most sense.

To start the conversation with a non-Christian, it may not be helpful to start with, "Do you believe Jesus is, 'The Way, The Truth, and the Life?'" That is where you want to end, but it is too complicated an idea to start with. Even telling someone, "Jesus Loves you" may not get you very far unless you can give some background on what that really means.

A great first question is, "Do you believe there is a spiritual dimension to reality?" There are two ways of helping people realize the beauty of the Christian message. The first is a direct comparison of the beliefs and creeds of Christianity to other spiritual worldviews. My first book, <u>Understanding the Spiritual Puzzle</u>, compares religions such as Hinduism, Buddhism, and Islam by looking at them as spiritual worldviews. In this book I will attempt to show the beauty of the good news of The Gospel by looking at Christianity from a historical perspective and how humanity developed a spiritual consciousness thanks to the teachings found in the Torah, and the words, actions, and teachings of Jesus. A great first step towards helping people understand Jesus is just informing them of the unequalled impact His teachings have had on the spiritual development of human society.

We will combine fresh ideas about history, psychology, philosophy, spirituality, and Christianity to help you understand how the individual consciousness and then the **spiritual consciousness** develops in humans. The human consciousness starts in a physical body, and then becomes a self-aware mind or psyche. Eventually, we realize we have a spiritual nature that is deeper than the mind. As individuals are developing their bodies, minds, and spirits, the culture also develops on a parallel and interdependent track. Just as the body, mind and spirit develop in each individual, the culture goes through three similar stages of development. The three stages of this social or cultural-spiritual development that parallel individual development are: Tribal, Intellectual, and Spiritual.

The parallel individual and social development tracks are shown here:

Individual: Body   Mind   Spirit
Cultural: Tribal   Intellectual Spiritual

All humans are born with a seed of spirituality. I call it spiritual, or God's DNA. All humans are born with spiritual DNA. We separate from our mothers, and we begin to realize and actualize our own individual personalities which are based around our individual ego and free will. Eventually, the ego can realize and actualize its spirit. The physical body eventually dies, but the spirit lives.

The Torah, which is the basis of the Judeo-Christian culture, believes humans were spiritually unified with God at one time. As a result of the free will God gave us, humans wanted to be independent from God's Will. We became **self-centered instead of God-centered**, so we became spiritually separated from the main source of our spirituality. Spiritual DNA has always been in us, but if it is not planted in fertile soil, it stays dormant.

Just like an acorn is separated from a tree and appears to be dead, but it comes back to life if it is put in fertile soil, our individual spirit can die if we do not nourish it and let it grow. Because of the Great Paradox of Human Existence, because humans were once primal or tribal beings, it has

4

taken thousands of years for humans to get to the point where we understand individually and collectively, **that we need to develop our spiritual being as well as our physical being**.

There is an interdependent relationship between the self and others. Humans take a much longer time to mature and begin to live on their own than any other animal. The nature of all education, or all forms of cognitive transformation or **intellectual growth is interdependence**. A baby begins in a crib and does not know the difference between itself and other people. Over time it begins to understand that it is different from other people. If a baby is left in a crib by itself, it does not learn anything. It must have social interaction with other people to learn. **The basis of all education is comparing what we know to what we do not know**. If we did not have other people and things different from us for comparison, we would never become smarter. Humans' intellectual progress sometimes moves fast and sometimes it moves slow. Individual spiritual development and progress are also very fluid. **All human knowledge is interdependent and cumulative**. It begins with an individual learning something and then that person teaches it to other people. Society progresses as different individuals think up different things and add to the collective knowledge. Together, a group, or a culture, or a nation of people, create something greater than the sum of each individual.

The Great Paradox of Human Existence

The great paradox of life is that humans are spiritual in nature, we have spiritual DNA, but it takes the human mind a while to understand its spirituality because we start as physical beings. We start as young humans and after a few years we develop an ego, which is our consciousness becoming self-conscious or conscious of our ability to interact with and affect the physical world. I believe *human existence is irrational*. The spiritual part of our existence is spiritual, it is not rational, it cannot be understood by reason alone. It is beyond reason. One of the many paradoxes of life is that it is logical to say human existence is irrational.

Hopefully, at some point, we become aware of our spiritual nature and that we are spirits that live in a body. Because the physical is so different from the spiritual, some people never progress beyond a physical or material understanding of reality. They never get to understand the **spiritual dimension of reality.** The goal of this book is to help Christians understand the Bible is God's story about the progress of the development of human spiritual consciousness. Individuals and society develop interdependently.

Presentism
Another problem many people are experiencing recently is *presentism*. Presentism is judging the past by the standards of the present. It is like saying you should have known at age ten what you now know at age fifty. Humans have an infinite number of faults and problems, but if we look at historical development, we can see great progress. With a proper understanding of the past, we can get an idea of where we are headed in the future.

Introduction Study Questions

Answers to questions are at the back of the book

Why is it good to understand how to describe Christianity in secular terms?

What is the Great Paradox of Human Existence?

What is the 'Nature of Education'?

Do you believe there are spiritual laws just like there are physical laws?

What is Presentism?

Chapter 1
Spiritual Consciousness Development

The first step of spiritual consciousness development is something everyone goes through, which is simply becoming conscious of yourself, or self-consciousness.

In the first few months of life, you begin to realize you are a separate physical being from other parts of the world. A baby's mind comes to consciousness by comparing itself to things to that are different than itself.

A baby can do nothing by itself. All humans are dependent on other humans to take care of them for many years. Humans are dependent on their parents much longer than other creatures. A baby's mind begins to understand the difference between the physical world around it, and itself. A baby develops language as it begins to make sounds and eventually name things that it can recognize. A child begins to talk as it learns about the world. It says, Mommy, Daddy, kitty, milk, etc. The first great day in any parents' life is when the child says Mommy, Daddy, or Papa.

Learning how to speak and to communicate with language is a beginning step in **realizing and actualizing your unique self**. It takes a few years to learn to reason and to think about things. I am not an expert in psychology, but those seem to be some of the first basic steps of ego development, or individual consciousness development.

The second step happens many years later when the mind becomes fully self-conscious or intellectually mature. At this stage you become aware you can **imaginatively recreate your environment and yourself**.

When you realize you have some control of your destiny, you become what I call *a self-aware I*. Psychologist Carl Jung calls this "self-realization". Before you become self-aware you are dependent on parents or caregiver(s) of some kind. The first steps to self-awareness can be as simple as building your own simple structure out of building blocks. A child can begin to express themselves by dressing in different ways or scribbling their own picture. Children do have good imaginations if they are encouraged. Maybe they want to change their room around or paint the walls or build a wagon. Eventually, a child matures and realizes they can help control their world through thought, speech, and action.

Words and actions are two ways the imagination or the spiritual world manifests into the physical world.

Eventually, a person becomes self-directed. They decide what classes to take in high school or college based on their hopes and dreams and goals. At some point parents or a counsellor will say, "You have to figure out what you are going to do with your life". At that point you realize you have to be a fully self-aware, self-directed unique individual trying to express your unique talents and personality.

The Third Step is spiritual consciousness awareness. After your ego matures, hopefully your mind becomes aware of the spiritual world and that you are also spiritual in nature. Spiritual consciousness can start before, during, or after you become a self-directed I.

The next BIG step is you develop your spiritual, or God consciousness. Some people are taught this early in life. Some people never develop a spiritual, or God consciousness, and many people succeed in the natural or physical world quite well without any spiritual consciousness. We will discuss reasons why people do or do not believe in God later in the book. However, it happens, at some point we begin to understand or feel, or have an awareness of a spiritual presence, or an intuition that there is something greater that exists beyond ourselves and the physical world.

An important step is when you realize spiritual instincts are different than natural instincts or your intellectual thoughts. This is very important, but it is something many people never understand.

Here are examples of the differences in what motivates you to act:

Your natural instinct tells you to hoard food and shelter for yourself and family.

Your intellect or reason says it is ok to share food with someone who can pay you back.

Your spiritual instinct or training tells you to help someone even though it does not benefit you and you may never get paid back.

In the book <u>Believing is Seeing</u>, scientist Michael Guillen talks about IQ and SQ. Your IQ is your intelligence quotient. Your SQ is your spiritual quotient, which is your awareness of, and sensitivity to, the spiritual part of reality. It is important to understand that just as we all have a biological or physical inheritance, there is a dimension of spiritual inheritance that comes along with the physical inheritance. Your spiritual quotient kicks in when your mind realizes that sometimes **your spiritual instincts must override your natural and rational instincts**. That is, your mind senses spiritual revelations are different, and better than your natural or rational instincts.

I call the next step the self-aware spiritual consciousness. Just like your consciousness became self-aware, your spirit matures to the point that it is a ***self- aware spirit.*** You begin to open up your Wi-Fi channel to God.

Many people call spiritual consciousness ***intuition***. One example is when someone calls you and you say, "I knew you were going to call". Another example is when you witness a miraculous healing that the Doctors can only explain as supernatural or beyond our understanding of the natural world.

You learn to develop your spiritual consciousness and communicate with a spiritual God, just like you learned to talk to your parents in the physical world. The most human, natural, or basic instinct is self-preservation. The self-preservation instinct causes you to want to understand yourself. The self-preservation instinct also causes you to want to know where you came from and where you are going. Most orphans have a deep desire to know where they came from.

Deep down below all of that you ALSO have an instinct to want to know the God who created you. Sometimes that instinct comes to the surface, sometimes it does not. As your spiritual consciousness becomes self-aware, you learn that natural instincts as well as some cultural and reasoned responses need to be overridden by spiritual instincts. You become spiritually mature just like you became intellectually mature.

One of the most difficult things to learn is that God's Presence, and God's Character, is beyond our ability to truly understand through reason, or describe with our language. It is especially hard in cultures that try to inhibit a human's spiritual desires and instincts.

The way we know God is through faith and love and a spiritual sensing **which is beyond human reason and human logic**. Faith and love are spiritual characteristics that transcend rational thought. If you confine yourself to traditional physical senses or material logic you will inhibit your ability to understand the spiritual dimension of reality.

Just like a child expresses mannerisms and physical characteristics of their physical parents, we begin to manifest characteristics of God due to a spiritual nature, or

God's DNA, that we are born with. Our spiritual characteristics must develop like all our other physical characteristics. God is our ultimate parent, so given the right time and environment we begin to express or manifest the attributes of God such as love, forgiveness, mercy, faith, patience, and kindness. The Creator is the essence and source of these non-rational attributes. Just like some people develop skills to be good at soccer or computer games or gymnastics, humans can develop their different spiritual abilities.

God is self-sufficient. He does not need us, but His DNA is in us. Just like any other talents or personality characteristics we have inherited, once we become aware of the spiritual part of our nature we can develop our spiritual awareness, knowledge, and instincts. As we develop the spiritual part of our being we realize and actualize our true essence, or our unique self.

The next step of spiritual consciousness development is when your spirit develops more than an intellectual understanding of the spiritual dimension of reality. It is a big move to begin to understand the spiritual dimension, but it is a bigger move to decide to develop a deeper relationship with God, and **to seriously consider the eternal implications of your spiritual nature.**

When you consider that God is the actual creative energy force at the beginning of Being, and that humans are part of the creation, then you realize it is impossible for a created being to be able to understand that which created it. We are only able to think in human terms. If we could know God in human terms, God would be less than human consciousness, but He is much, much, more.

The difficult part to understand is that God transcends our ability to understand Him, (or Her). At some point, our spirit realizes and actualizes an innate relationship with God. Your spirit is the DNA link between us and God that is beyond your reason.

There are three phases to individual development: physical, intellectual, then spiritual. You start in a physical body, then your mind matures and eventually many people get to the point where they intellectually realize there is a spiritual dimension. At that point, you realize you can begin using your *spiritual Wi-Fi connection to God* you are born with.

God's DESIGN is for God's image, God's DNA, or God's Love, to manifest itself through each individual. There are over sixty trillion cells in your body, and your body and mind are a unique combination of physical and spiritual components. Obviously, at the current stage of human development we are living in, we understand the physical dimension much better than the spiritual dimension of our existence.

The self-aware, spiritually conscious self begins to understand how God's image, God's Spirit, or God's DNA is expressed through each human.

Your spiritual consciousness must overcome many natural and culturally induced instincts. To allow God's DNA, or your spiritual essence, to flourish, you have to strip away all the cultural and natural baggage that is tightly connected to, and possibly psychologically dependent on, the material world. We need to change our spiritual diet from sugar and snacks and caffeine to pure spiritual protein, so to speak.

Your natural instincts take your mind to the level of your consciousness. Your mind helps you realize your spiritual nature, but then your mind has to allow your spiritual instincts to take you to the level of your spiritual consciousness.

The next step in developing a deeper relationship with God is like **the difference between knowing someone and marrying someone**. When you are married, you incorporate the other person into all parts of your life. You talk to them constantly. You discuss actions and relate to others as a couple not just a single person. You consider your spouse in all that you do. If you have a true love relationship their "Being" indwells you, you sense their being inside of you. You know how they will think or react. All relevant decisions are made considering your spouse.

Learning how to relate to God is a process just like learning to relate to other humans. It takes many interactions to get to know someone. When you go through many different situations together you come to know them better and you know how they will react. Ultimately, we are trying to have a relationship with something that created us. We are trying to understand how to relate to the being that created our ability to reason. We can never fully know God rationally, that is why we must depend on faith and love, and spiritual instincts. We depend on senses that are trans-logical, that transcend logic and reason. We depend on a spiritual connection.

What I have just described in secular terms is what Christians call being *born again*. It is when you confess with your words and believe in your spirit that Jesus gave His life to redeem the rest of humanity. When you come to that realization you have moved from being motivated by reason and intelligence to being spiritually conscious and being motivated by God and your spiritual intuition.

Faith and love are the magnifying glass and prism that allow you to understand God and allow you to manifest the spiritual into the physical world. Faith is a concept that takes a lot of explanation, and we will discuss it in a later chapter. For now, we will say, just like a magnifying glass can create a flame from energy you cannot see, our faith brings God's Will into physical reality. Faith changes spiritual ideas into physical realities.

God has energy and spirit that you can tap. Our intellect takes us far, but ultimately, we need to leap beyond the intellectual to the spiritual. We need to step from the logical, physical world into the trans-logical world of the transcendent reality.

If your faith is like a magnifying glass, your love is like a prism. If you put a prism in the sun, you see a rainbow. Your ability to love is like a prism. It takes God's energy that you cannot see and breaks it up into all the beautiful parts so you can see all the beauty it contains. **The prism of your unique personal love transforms God's spirit or energy into a beautiful array of ideas, words, actions and emotions**. Your faith and your love are part rational and part spiritual. They are part natural, part supernatural, and part emotions or feelings. That is why they are hard to describe.

Ultimately, when you become a self-aware spirit and you realize there are many spiritual worldviews, then you need to use your mind and your spirit to sort through them and decide what you think is true. For more about the subject of comparative worldviews, check out my book <u>Understanding the Spiritual Puzzle</u>, <u>Comparing Spiritual Worldviews</u>, where I compare all the major spiritual worldviews.

Once you have decided there is a spiritual dimension to reality, and you are a spirit that lives in a body, then you need to sort out just exactly what that means.

You can never fully know God, but your faith and your spiritual sensing can take you where your rational mind cannot.

The truth, and a great deal of spiritual knowledge or wisdom that lasts, can only be learned spiritually with the help of your faith. Spirituality transcends physical reality, so your mind must think beyond the physical to understand the spiritual. Some scientists refer to this as ***translogical.***

Michael Guillen is a contemporary scientist who grew up in the barrios of Los Angeles. He went to Cornell University and eventually taught at Harvard. Michael became a world class scientist, trained in ivy league physics, astrophysics, astronomy, and mathematics. He is a gifted communicator who became a well know journalist and an Emmy award winner. In his book <u>Believing is Seeing</u> he says we have to be able to think beyond what we know to be rational because, "what we're able to prove the existence of—is only a small fraction of what's out there". Guillen goes on to say translogical thinking is the most penetrating way of seeing, probing, and describing the universe. In a sense, it's a superpower unique to the human species; no other animal on the planet is capable of it. Far more sophisticated than mere IQ, **translogical thinking is a special kind of intelligence** -- one that transcends the pedestrian rules of Aristotelian logic. You are capable of translogical thinking, and so am I. But, tragically, not everyone uses it in daily life -- or even knows they have the ability for it.[2]

A more basic way to describe translogical thinking is to say just like electricity only flows through certain substances (copper and metal but not wood or stone) God's truth can only flow to you and through you if your mind is open to thinking outside the physical, or the logical, box.

The heart is generally considered the center of the person. The term follow your heart means follow what is at the center of your individual being. I translate the term heart to spirit. So, when people say follow your heart, they are saying follow your spirit or your spiritual nature.

The final step of spiritual consciousness development is when God's Spirit indwells in you. You realize you can never understand God in human terms, but you decide you are going to let the spirit of God indwell in you. We will get into what that looks like and how it works later. For the purposes of this chapter, we are just trying to understand ALL the different steps of spiritual consciousness development. If you totally embrace spirituality this is where you end up, regardless of your spiritual worldview. Some Christians call this relationship with God being **Spirit filled.**

Spiritual maturity doesn't happen quickly, like physical maturity it doesn't happen overnight, it can take years or a full lifetime. Think of the indwelling Spirit as the difference between having God as a friend or being married to God. The final analogy is when you eat food, it nourishes you, it gives you energy and literally becomes part of you. When you become spirit filled the spirit nourishes you spiritually.

When you get married to God, when you are conscious of God's indwelling spirit, your life is changed. You develop a spiritual or supernatural connection with God.

A spiritual awakening is when you are walking and talking with God regularly just like you do with your spouse. Your spirit tries to stay aligned with God's spirit. Your spirit, words, and actions, become in line with God's Will. You realize God's direction and God's timing comes from within regardless of what you hear and see all around you.

Another way of understanding this is to say you realize that however the Universe was created it was created with a great deal of order. Our roles as human beings are to try to the best of our abilities, to understand that order, and how our unique talents fit in that order.

The Hindus talk about Moksha. Buddhists and secular thinkers talk about Enlightenment. The Muslims talk about getting to Paradise. Christians say God came to earth to show us how a spirit filled or spiritually motivated being actually talks and acts.

Through faith and love you let God show Himself to you to the best of your ability to understand Him.

We do not need to get God to listen to us, we need to open that sixth sense and listen to God.

However brightly God's light may shine, it can only be seen by those who are prepared to see it. Unless we have the magnifying glass of faith, or the prism of love, we never manifest the full power and energy of God.

The sun shines on a piece of paper all day, but when you put a magnifying glass in between the paper and the sun, it creates a physical flame. Your faith in God transforms the energy you cannot see into a flame.

So, this briefly describes what I call spiritual consciousness development. We are all at different stages of this process.

Chapter 1 Study Questions

How does a baby begin to process information?

What does it mean to be a 'Self-aware I'?

What are two ways the spiritual world manifests itself into the physical world?

Describe the difference between natural/instinctual, rational, and spiritual motivations for actions?

What does it mean to be spiritually 'self-aware'?

What is meant by Faith is like a magnifying glass?

What is meant by your Love is like a prism?

Does it make sense to say a created being can understand the Creator?

What is meant by God's DNA?

How is getting to know God like getting to know a friend?

What does it mean to be *married to God*?

Do you believe The Spirit of God can dwell in you?
	Only you can answer this question.

Chapter 2
Three Stages of Individual and Social Development

As we try to understand the development of spiritual consciousness, it is important to understand that social progress and individual development are interdependent, cumulative, and progressive. Einstein was able to develop quantum physics because he learned Newtonian physics first. We have Wi-Fi today because people invented the radio and TV first. We have computers and cell phones because someone figured out how to turn sand into glass and then into computer chips.

There is an interdependent relationship between the individual and society.

Just as the individual goes from understanding the body, then the mind, then the spirit, a society starts out as a primal/tribal group, and eventually becomes organized based on reason and rules. Ultimately, the hope is the society gets to a point where the culture is motivated by spiritual understanding.

We will continue to discuss the three stages of human individual and social development:

Individual -	Body	Mind/Psyche	Spirit
Social -	Tribal	Ideological	Spiritual

Humans take much longer to mature and live independently than other animals.

All education is based on comparing what you know to what you do not know. A baby in a crib does not learn anything until it is taken outside the crib and is exposed to things different from itself. Part of our continuing to grow is helping to maintain the conditions for other people to be different from us. Without that we cannot continue to grow. Our **growth is dependent on a diverse population around us**.

Earlier we mentioned the great paradox, that is, our physical body develops before our spiritual consciousness. Because of this paradox some people, unfortunately, never come to a true realization that they are spiritual in nature.

Three phases of Social Development

The first phase of social development is the Primal/ Tribal/ Emotional/ Traditional culture. Primal humans walk out of the cave, and they are faced with the **Omnipotent Unknown.** Primal humans must be intensely negative and defensive. They spend all their time trying to understand and anticipate all the bad things that can cause them harm. Humans in the early tribes do not have a strong sense of self. They are a group motivated by hunger and fear. If someone from their group is killed it is just what happens to part of the group. They move on and continue to try and survive. They are driven by emotions, instincts, and traditions. Before fire, tools, and the wheel, they spend all their time rummaging for food. The strongest person rules by force.

Men are more adventurous and aggressive because for most of the time, humans were on the earth the men had to find food. Women are more compassionate and more negative because their primary concern is protecting and caring for the children. They have to anticipate all the negative things that could happen to the child.

The Second Phase of individual human intellectual development was started by the philosophical thinking and writings of **Socrates**. Dr. Peter Kreft is a well-known Philosophy Professor at Boston College. He recently authored a series of books and lectures called <u>Socrate's Children</u>. Dr. Kreft makes the assertion that Socrates was the world's first Philosopher and logical thinker, and the first human to claim a quest for wisdom. He was the first human to define his terms clearly and prove his concepts logically. Socrates birthed the age of reason and he tiptoed into the

Third phase of human consciousness development which is spiritual thinking when he claimed the soul was more important than the body. Socrates was martyred for his beliefs and his refusal to honorably profess that he believed in the gods of the state. What Socrates started, Plato and Aristotle continued. Aristotle is called the Father of Science.

Socrates never wrote anything. Plato was the student of Socrates who did all the writing, so it is a little difficult to know who actually thought of what. The student started with what he learned from Socrates and then reasoned his way into an understanding of spirituality. Plato believed that the difference between humans and animals was the ability to do abstract thinking or reason. He said Reason rises above sensation and knows the Universal essence of things. He believed that forms or essences or universal truths were objective reality. People refer to Platonic ideas as unchanging perfect standards. Socrates began to understand the Form of God but NOT the person of God. One could argue that Plato laid the foundation of Reason that helped humans transition to the third stage of Spiritual Consciousness Development.

Socrates was the father of Reason and therefore, the father of the second phase of individual human consciousness development. The second phase of social development is basing the laws of society on Ideologies and not the whim of a King or Emperor or the physically strongest person. The Greeks invented and flirted with Democracy and the rule of law, but it wasn't until the Reformation, the Renaissance, and the Industrial Revolution that humans even began to get serious about organizing societies along ideological lines. Even in the 1600's most countries were run by Kings or Emperors.

For most of history except for Israel, the major nations were all ruled by the traditions of the strongest family's rule, with an eye for an eye mentality. The Magna Carta was written in 1200s and was revived in the 1500s. The basis of the Magna

Carta was that all men should be treated equally under the law. This was the beginning of people thinking about basing the laws of a country on ideology as opposed to the power of the strongest or the traditions of the monarchy. The monarchy in France ended during the French Revolution in 1793 when Louis the XVI was executed. The Democratic movement started in 1832 in England when the First Reform act was passed but full voting rights for men and women over the age of 18 was not passed until 1969.

The third phase of social development is Spirituality Organized Societies. The nation of Israel was the only nation founded on spiritual principles or the Laws of a Creator Personal God before 1700. Jerusalem was sacked in 70 AD and the Jews were dispersed throughout the world. The Nation of Israel went through many transitions over the next nineteen hundred years. It was ruled by the pagan Romans, the Persians, Byzantines, Muslim Caliphs, Crusaders, and the Ottomans to name a few. The British captured Jerusalem from the Ottomans in WWI. The country of Israel was reinstated by the British in 1948 when the British withdrew after World War II. It must be considered a miracle, or an amazing spiritual act, that a country promised to Abraham by God around 1900 BC would be reinstated 3800 years after it was last taken over by many different hateful foreign powers.

We will discuss the amazing formation of modern democracies and spiritually organized countries later in the book.

Now that we have an overview of individual consciousness development, and social organization structures, we will go back and review ancient history and cultures and work our way through history to better understand the history *of spiritual consciousness development.*

Chapter 2 Study Questions

Are humans independent or Interdependent?

What are the three stages of individual development?

What are the three stages of social development?

When did many countries begin to transition from Monarchies to democracies?

When did a nation other than Israel become spiritually organized?

Stay tuned.

Chapter 3
Ancient Gods, Abraham, and Moses

It is generally agreed that a conception of a god or a spiritual worldview is expected to explain four things:

Creation–How did the world begin?
Morality–What is right and what is wrong?
Meaning–What gives your life meaning?
The Future–What does your Spiritual Worldview prophesy or indicate the gods will do in the future?

To understand the beginning of **social spiritual consciousness development,** we will start with a discussion of the ancient gods. It is very difficult to describe ancient religions or Hinduism or Buddhism because they were started and flourished for thousands of years in illiterate cultures. As of 1947 when India was ruled by the British, it was comprised of over twenty territories with over twenty different languages. Most people were illiterate and there were very few phones for long distance communication. People in North India had very different ideas about the gods than people in South India. The cultures where Buddhism was founded and thrived throughout India, China and Thailand were also very diverse and illiterate. It was not until the last fifty years and modern communications, primarily the cell phone, that Buddhists or Hindus in one area began to compare themselves to people with the same religious beliefs in other areas.

The same is true of the gods of ancient cultures. Each local tribe or culture had explanations for the origin of the universe and how to explain the paralyzing fear of the unknown, but the ideas were all regional and very different. The various powers of the gods explained the origins of the universe as well as natural phenomena like storms (lightning bolts from Zeus), volcanoes (the inner world coughing or fighting), or floods and plagues which were sent by an upset god to punish people. Sometimes these natural disasters were thought to be the result of a war between gods.

Edith Hamilton in her book <u>Mythology</u> says, "the early gods **had no semblance of reality**. They were unlike all living things. Egypt had a towering colossus, immobile, beyond the power of the imagination to endow with movement, as fixed in the stone as the tremendous temple columns. A representation of the human shape deliberately made unhuman. Or a rigid figure, a woman with a cat's head suggesting inflexible, inhuman cruelty. Or a monstrous mysterious sphinx, aloof from all that lives. In Mesopotamia, bas-reliefs of bestial shapes unlike any beast ever known, men with birds' heads and lions with bulls' heads and both with eagles' wings, creations of artists who were intent upon producing something never seen except in their own minds, the very consummation of unreality."[1] Many early gods were projections of the imagination, or subconsciousness, or the worst fears of the people. The individuals with the greatest imaginations were oftentimes considered the sorcerers or priests and they were given power as they tried to explain the gods.

If one tribe conquered another tribe, the conquered people who survived were expected to begin to worship the gods of the victors so that the gods would not be mad and would continue to help them be victorious. It is said, one of the reasons the Romans persecuted and killed Christians is because the Roman Emperors felt the Christians worshipped the wrong gods and if that was allowed to continue it would make their gods mad. Natural disasters and storms or floods were the result of punishment by the gods or fighting between the gods.

Hamilton also points out that during the Greek enlightenment period, the Greek gods became more humanized. The gods went from half man, half animals, or creatures of the imagination, to the more idealized human gods of Hercules, Venus, Apollo, and Neptune.

The gods of the ancient cultures varied from tribe to tribe. They were a mix of projections of fears and imaginations, myths, mystical thinking. They combined traits of humans and animals and were oftentimes considered to be acting on human emotions.

Abraham & Moses, and the Chosen people
The story of Abraham is a historic development in the history of the spiritual development of humanity. As we have just pointed out, for the most part, all cultures in the world were highly polytheistic, and based on tradition and survival of the fittest. Out of nowhere, amidst hundreds of gods, comes Abraham who **hears the voice of a singular personal God.** The first instruction from God to Abraham is to leave his home, his country, and his extended family. God instructed Abraham to **abandon his key traditions** and the practices of the culture of his ancestors.

It is difficult to imagine how hard this must have been. In today's Western Infotech based society, we experience change at a rapid pace. In 2000 BC, the culture changed very slowly. An interesting question to think about is did God try to talk to other humans, but Abraham was the only one that listened? Whatever the reason, Abraham was the first person since Noah who listened to God and began to structure his life and his family's lives around instructions from God instead of the primal emotional traditions of the society into which he was born.

Abraham began the FIRST, God (spiritually) conscious, or spiritually organized family and then culture or society. He demonstrated his commitment to God or his faith in God by continually being willing to sacrifice his possessions and even his son to the God whose voice he heard.

Abraham and his ancestors struggled mightily trying to live according to God's instructions, or God's word, or spiritual motivation, and not be subject to the same whims and instinctual pleasures as other cultures. The cultures of Abraham's day were driven by the traditions of an eye for an eye, or to the most powerful belongs the spoils. Child sacrifice, raping women, enslaving men, pillaging the treasure of those you conquered, and parading the spoils was standard procedure. As we know from the days of the Roman Coliseum that came many years later, watching slaves battle slaves, watching men battle beasts, and watching beasts battle beasts to the death, was considered great fun. Certainly, Abraham and his followers had their work cut out for them as they tried to create a different culture for their family.

When God interacted with humans, he did it with a series of Covenants. This is the practice God used with Adam, Noah, Abraham, and subsequently with Moses and David. God made a Covenant with Abraham, whose original name was Abram, and his family. In Genesis 12, the Lord said to Abram, "Go from your country, your people and your father's household to the land I will show you". **This is God telling Abraham he must leave his cultural Traditions!** God told Abraham if he would leave his old ways, "I will make you into a great nation, and I will bless you; I will make your name great, and you will be a blessing. I will bless those who bless you, and whoever curses you I will curse; and all peoples on earth will be blessed through you."

After many years Abraham did not have any children and he began to doubt God's Covenant that he would be the father of many nations. This is an example of how personal the God of Abraham was. Abraham tells God he has waited many years and he does not have offspring finally in 15:5 it says, "He (God) took him outside and said, 'Look at the sky, and count the stars - if indeed you can count them.' And He said to him, "So shall your offspring be." Verse 6 says **"Abraham believed in the Lord, and He** (The Lord) **credited it to him** (Abraham) **as righteousness** (being in right standing with the Lord)."

This was the first instance since Noah and the destruction of the Earth **that someone acted according to God's instructions instead of tradition or to appease a pagan god.** There was no physical indication that Abraham who was over 100 years old at that point, and his wife Sarah, who had been barren all her life and was well past the age of childbearing could have a child. Verse six says if you act according to God's instruction, regardless of the physical circumstances then you are righteous or in right standing with God. **This was the beginning of a culture or nation based on the words of, and faith in, a singular, personal Creator God.** Abraham is said to be chosen because he listened to God. A secular interpretation is, Abraham became the first spiritually consciousness human because he was driven by spiritual instincts or feelings not by cultural traditions.

Abraham became the bearer of the ancestral genealogy of the people of Israel. It is fascinating to realize there were very few steps between Adam and Abraham. Biblical history tells us there were about 2,000 years between Adam and Abraham, but because the people lived so long, they were only four generations apart.

The history of the families between Abraham and Moses is very interesting but for the sake of this work we will talk about Moses next. The descendants of Abraham ended up as slaves to the Egyptians. Moses was the next major figure to listen and hear the voice of God. Like Abraham, Moses had a very personal relationship with God. Moses led the descendants of Abraham to escape from captivity with God's help. The spiritual lesson here is that if you listen to God, He can help you change your situation. He wants you to be free to worship Him, and He will help you become free if you listen to Him.

Moses–Social Spiritual Organization
After Moses lead the Hebrews out of slavery in Egypt, he had the unenviable job of structuring a new nation from a

group of people who had been slaves for 400 years. When a culture has been in captivity for that long they have to start from scratch to construct new social and political systems. They had nothing to begin with. Fortunately, Moses was spiritually attentive, and God gave him ten commandments to begin to build a social framework. **This was the first time a tribe, or culture, or nation organized itself based on the laws of God or, Spiritual Laws instead of tradition and the laws of the most powerful men in the tribe.**

Moses also wrote the history of his people. The oral tradition was passed down from Adam to Methuselah, to Noah and Shem, to Abraham, then Isaac, Jacob, Levi and Amram to Moses.

There were lots of lessons in the Book of Genesis, which is the information Moses had to work with as he tried to lead his people to become the great nation that God promised to Abraham. We will discuss the basics of the spiritual world God described to Moses:

- o Sin is separation from God
    - It is being self- centered, or material centered, **not God-centered.**
- o A Singular Personal God created the world in perfect order
    - God gave dominion to humans.
- o Humans are created in **the image of God**
- o Individuals and nations must follow the Laws of God not the laws of Humans

Two interesting take aways about the world god created are:

- The only thing out of order in today's world is human Free will.
- **God honors your Free Will more than He desires a sinless world.**

Genesis illustrates the concept that sin is separation from God. Sin is being self-centered and choosing to exercise your free will that is contrary to God's Will. As we have said earlier, primal tribal cultures are based on emotion and tradition and a very physical worldview, so trying to get his fellow humans to be God-Centered and obeying spiritual laws was very difficult for Moses. There are many examples when the Hebrew people would revert to worshipping golden calves or other pagan idols while Moses was trying to get them to listen to God.

The next thing that is different than any other ideas of the time was that a singular, personal God created everything, and He gave humans dominion over all the earth. The ancient cultures believed the pagan gods created and controlled the earth and humans just had to try to keep the gods happy. No other pagan worldviews had such a simple worldview. Moses's version explained that God created a man and woman in Paradise and told them they were blessed with all blessings and there was only one temptation they had to worry about. God explained to Adam that he could do anything except eat the fruit from the tree of good and evil. The tree was a symbol of human's free will choice.

Life could not have been easier than their life in the Garden of Eden. It shows that God created humans with Free Will and God honors your Free Will more than he wants a sinless world. The story of Adam and Eve tells us that when we are God-centered, and we walk and talk with God, and we follow God's rules, we are in paradise. Unfortunately, the first humans could not stay spiritually centered or God-centered. If there is only one temptation in the whole world it seems humans will succumb to that one temptation. When Eve and Adam ate the fruit that God told them not to eat, they took the **first self-centered action.** They exercised their Free will against God's will. Sin is being self-centered or centered on the physical world instead of being God centered or centered on the spiritual world and spiritual laws.

Another basic lesson of Genesis is that God has created everything in perfect order. If you look outward at the sun, the moon, and the stars, or inward at the miraculous way the human body works, you see incredible complexity and order and balance. **The only part of nature that is out of order is human free will**. What Moses knew that was difficult to explain to others was that the key to life was understanding and following God's will and God's order and not the traditions and laws of primal tribal cultures of the time.

Another "gem" that was buried in the first few chapters of Genesis was the concept that humans are created in the image of God. It is hard to know if even Moses understood the full impact of this phrase and it took thousands of years for humanity to fully understand what it meant for humans to be created in the Image of God. We will discuss that in the next chapter.

Chapter 3 Study Questions

What four things must a Spiritual Worldview explain?

What were the early gods like?

Why was Abraham "Chosen"?

What was the first thing God told Abraham to do?

Why does the author say Abraham was the father of social Spiritual Consciousness?

How does Genesis describe Sin?

Does God honor your Free Will if you choose to do evil?

Was Abraham the only person that God tried to speak to?

Chapter 4
The Image of God

In the first chapter of the Bible is one of the most important and transformative statements in the history of human spiritual consciousness development. Genesis is certainly one of the oldest and most studied books in the history of humanity. Genesis 1:26 says, *"Then God said: Let us make mankind in our **image**, in our **likeness**."* I interpret this to say that since God is a spirit, humans also have a spiritual component, or a spiritual nature, or even that we are spirits that live in a body.

According to the Merriam Webster Dictionary, *image* means representation of the external form. This means that humans represent God in external form. If we represent God in human form, it certainly means we have a spiritual component. Ancient gods were projections or imaginations, primarily of what humans feared. The God of Abraham and Moses told us God presents Himself through us. We all have a splash of the divine inside us. We have **spiritual DNA just like we have physical DNA**. Because of the Great Paradox of Human Existence, it is hard for many people to turn that splash of the Divine into a "fountain of living water".

The first chapter of Genesis, including the statement about created in the image of God, begins to answer all four of the questions a spiritual worldview should answer.

Creation: God. The ultimate Spirit created everything, including humans. Humans have dominion over everything.

Meaning: We are meant to represent God's Image.

Morality: God is Sovereign and deserves all respect and honor. If ALL humans are created in God's Image then ALL humans deserve respect and honor and should be treated with respect and honor. All people should be treated as fully sovereign humans.

Future: If we are spirits that live in a body then somehow our spirits will continue to exist once the body is no longer in existence.

Another interesting Biblical statement that further defines the Image of God is John 1:1 that tells us "In the beginning was the Word, and the Word was with God, and the Word was God." Some scholars also translate 'Word' to 'Logos' which can mean reason or consciousness or *Being*. Also, words are ways the spiritual world is manifested into the physical world. When John says, "in the beginning was the Word", that means God is manifesting Himself into the physical world. Jesus is considered the first human physical manifestation of God on the earth, so Jesus was the Word, but if we humans are also representations of God, we are also words of God and our reason and our consciousnesses are meant to represent God.

Another deep connection is that humans are the only beasts that can speak words. Our linguistic ability is part of the uniqueness or image of God. It is an expression of our consciousness and our reason or our logos.

John 1:4 goes on to say, "in Him was Life, and the life was the light of all mankind. The light shines in the darkness, and the darkness has not overcome it". This means that Jesus was life, which means spiritual life, and he was the light of all men. He brought Spiritual Light to all people. As we will discuss in the next chapter, **Jesus was the first human that tried to explain spirituality to humanity.** Because of the *Great Paradox* of *Human Existence*, most humans could not understand what Jesus was trying to teach about the Image of God that is in all of us.

The best way to explain the *Image of God* to non-Christians is to say Christians believe all humans are unique sovereign individuals. Each individual deserves respect, and each individual has a responsibility to realize and actualize the unique gifts God gave each of us.

Moses to Jesus

Before we got distracted talking about the Image of God, we were talking about Moses trying to organize a nation built on the laws of the God of Abraham, not the laws of men. There were approximately fifteen hundred years between Moses and Jesus. In that time the Hebrews made it to the promised land, they started courts to enforce the laws, they selected Kings, and they won some battles and lost some battles. They struggled mightily, individually and as a group, to understand what it meant to live by, and run a nation by, the laws of God. They were unique among all cultures in their intermittent pursuit of a personal relationship with the one true personal God.

The last Book of the Old Testament was written about 400 BC. That would be the last God was heard of for four hundred years. In that time, the Jews began writing more laws of men than concentrating on the Laws of God. The Jews wrote the Talmud which began to deviate from God's Will for the Chosen Nation. Many Rabbis became corrupt and were more worried about selling animals and charging a commission on sacrifices of grain, animals, and money, than they were about the true spiritual condition or the relationship of their believers to God.

The story of Adam and Eve eating the forbidden fruit tells us that humans are sinful; in that they choose their own free will over the Will of God, and no matter how much they want to understand God they were struggling with the whole concept of spirituality.

Humanity has been spiritually separated from God since God cursed Adam and Eve and removed them from the shadow of His blessing, which is described as removing them from the garden of Eden. Thousands of years after humans separated themselves from God, He gave the Nation of Israel laws in the form of Ten Commandments. Israel struggled to obey the laws and they really struggled to have any deep understanding of spirituality, or of God's spiritual nature. It was time for the next step in the spiritual consciousness development of humanity.

Chapter 4 Study Questions

What does it mean to be created in the image of God?

What does it mean when John said "In the beginning was the Word, and the Word was God, and the Word was with God??

(See chapter 6 for a better explanation of the
Godhead or Trinity)

Chapter 5
Jesus, the first Human Rights advocate

All legitimate historians believe Jesus of Nazareth was a true historical figure. Whether or not you believe the Christian idea that Jesus was the Son of God, or the redeemer of humanity, anyone who studies human history, and especially the history of human spiritual development, will understand that Jesus of Nazareth had a more profound impact on the spiritual development of humanity than anyone else in human history.

Anyone who appreciates history, or the psychology of human social relationships, cannot help but understand the huge, significant change Jesus had on humanity in a secular as well as a religious sense.

Jesus was born into the Jewish culture when Israel was occupied by Rome. Pompey conquered Jerusalem in 67 BC. Previously, the Jewish people had been slaves for four hundred years under Egypt. They developed their own nation for many years. They were conquered and restored and conquered again. At the coliseum people would cheer as they watched men fight men to death. It was a totally brutal eye for an eye and tooth for a tooth culture, and the traditions, customs, and protocols were stifling. The Romans allowed the Jewish people to practice their own religion as long as they paid their taxes to Caesar. People of that time were born, they lived, and they died becoming what the culture expected them to become. Your ability to exercise your free will or realize and actualize your unique personality or talents was almost nonexistent.

Jesus provided a totally new perspective on human rights and personal freedom based on God's laws or spiritual laws, NOT on accepted cultural norms. Jesus's teachings were one hundred and eighty degrees different from what anyone at the time had ever heard of or could imagine, and that includes most of his own Jewish Nation.

Jewish culture had a strong sense of history and destiny due to their written history. The Jewish culture, like many other people groups were used to being dominated by a more powerful and brutal government. They prayed and hoped for a military leader who could rally the people to overthrow the Roman army powerfully and violently. They were lost, as was all of humanity, in a physical only worldview where God or spirituality was not taken seriously as a part of life. At best their concept of God was a disciplining parent that showed up to scold and punish.

Until the time of Jesus, no one in history had ever talked about forgiveness, grace, love of others, or actions that were a result of spiritual laws or God's Word.

As mentioned earlier there were many great spiritual laws or teachings from God in Genesis but any non-traditional actions based on spiritual ideas other than the Ten Commandments had been lost over the years.

From a secular historical perspective, it is obvious that Jesus was the **First Human Rights Advocate.** Another way to describe Jesus in secular terms is the first, self-realized spirit in human history.

Women's Rights
Jesus was one of the first documented Women's Rights Advocates. In Luke 10:40, The Bible tells the story of Martha and Mary, Lazarus's sisters. Martha was busy with the domestic chores and Mary was sitting with Jesus and some disciples. Mary was not helping with the domestic chores which made Martha upset so she said to Jesus, "Lord, don't you care that my sister has left me to do the work by myself? Tell her to help me!" "Martha, Martha," the Lord answered, "you are worried and upset about many things, but few things are needed -- or indeed only one. Mary has chosen what is better, and it will not be taken away from her."

This is the first time in human history that a woman was known to sit at the feet of a Rabbi, and to spend time discussing spiritual things with men instead of helping with domestic chores. Jesus let Martha and the rest of the world know that sitting at His feet and listening to Him talk about the Kingdom of God is the one thing we should be doing that is more important than anything else. It was the beginning of the Women's Rights movement, the Human Rights movement, and one of several instances where a man in authority and especially a Rabbi said it was OK for a woman to sit with Rabbis and talk about God. Until that time, everyone thought like Martha, that a woman's place was taking care of the men and the house, not sitting as equals of men discussing God. Jesus was trying to help humans understand that knowledge of spiritual laws and the laws of God, is more important than knowing physical laws. The point of the encounter is that we are **All Equal** and important at the feet of Jesus.

At Jesus's time in history a woman's opinion or testimony was never considered credible. When Jesus's body was found missing at the tomb after His crucifixion, He appeared to Mary Magdalene. She went and told the disciples about the missing body and her testimony was considered credible. When Jesus met Mary Magdalene, she was demon possessed. So not only was this one of the first times in recorded history that a woman's testimony was listened to and considered credible, but it was also a woman who had recovered from mental illness. Without Jesus showing that He loved her, and He wanted her well, no other man would have ever associated with her, much less believed her testimony.

Children's Rights

In Jesus' time children were considered property. Many cultures sacrificed children and many women of all ages were abused with impunity. Jesus was one of the first humans to treat children as fully human.

Matthew 19:13 says, "Then people brought little children to Jesus for him to place his hands on them and pray for them. But the disciples rebuked them." Jesus said, "Let the little children come to me, and do not hinder them, for the kingdom of heaven belongs to such as these."[15] "When he had placed his hands on them, he went on from there." This is the part of Jesus's teaching where He lets people know that children should also be treated as fully human.

Jesus takes a stand against scapegoating and hypocritical judgement and forgives a woman caught in adultery.

In John 8:1-6 the Pharisees tried to trap Jesus when they brought him a woman caught in adultery. They reminded Jesus that the Law of Moses said a woman caught in adultery should be stoned. The scripture then says, "they kept on questioning him, he straightened up and said to them, "Let any one of you who is without sin be the first to throw a stone at her." Again, he stooped down and wrote on the ground. At this, those who heard began to go away one at a time, the older ones first, until only Jesus was left, with the woman still standing there. Jesus straightened up and asked her, "Woman, where are they? Has no one condemned you?" "No one, sir," she said, "Then neither do I condemn you," Jesus declared. "Go now and leave your life of sin."

Jesus did not say go and do more deeds to make up for the bad deeds you have done. He simply said, "leave your life of sin". Like many of Jesus' ideas, forgiving an adulterer was something no one had ever considered before. Most people have not been taught that Jesus was the first human in history who taught about forgiveness.

Forgiveness

In addition to being the first well known Human Rights advocate, **Jesus Christ was the first human to introduce**

and promote the concept of forgiveness, including forgiveness of enemies, and eventually forgiveness of sins. In John Ortberg's book <u>Who is this Man</u>, the author points out that before Jesus, in Rome, **the prayer tablets were "curse tablets"**. The most common type of prayer was a curse. People would give the name of someone who hurt them, tell what their crime was, then specify how they wanted the gods to harm them. The prayers to Zeus and Bacchus asked the gods to punish one's enemies. **There were no prayers that asked the gods to forgive one's enemies or bless one's enemies**. [1]

Jesus was citing conventional wisdom in Matthew 5:43 when he noted "You have heard that it was said, 'Love your neighbor and hate your enemy, but I say to you love your enemies and pray for those who curse you'". Literature professor **David Konstan, a well-respected classics professor at Brown and NYU,** said that, "Forgiveness as we know it did not exist in ancient Greece and Rome."[2]

Noted historian **Hannah Arendt,** the first woman appointed to a full professorship at Princeton University, said, **"Forgiveness and love of enemies is a distinctly Christian contribution to humanity.**"[3]

Those are examples from three noted historians who all agree **the concept of forgiveness was awakened to human consciousness by Jesus and His followers.**

Today the concept of forgiveness is a common idea. In Matthew 5:46, it was Jesus who first said. "If you love (only) those who love you, what reward will you get? Are not even the tax collectors doing that?" **Jesus's whole ministry was about a radical awakening of the concepts of love, forgiveness, spiritual understanding, and treating all people as equal humans.** When Jesus's ministry started, no one in the world was talking about any of these concepts.

Let's discuss some examples:

The parable of the prodigal son as Jesus told it in Luke 15:11-32 **was stunningly different from the Hebrew version that existed before Jesus.** In the traditional version when the prodigal son came home to his father after being away with Gentiles, the father and other townspeople would meet the prodigal son on the road where they would break a pot to symbolize their broken relationship. The father or someone in the community would say, "You have shamed the family and you have shamed the community, go away, you are not part of the family anymore. You are dead to us." This is the Hebrew ceremony called **Kezazah.** [4]

Jesus was the author of the radical revision of this tradition. Jesus changed the story, so the father ran out to his son, and he was there to take the shame on himself. He forgave the son before anyone from the town would see him.

The father interceded to accept any shame for his son. Then the father accepted the son back into his house and threw a party and celebrated because the "lost" son was now found. **No one had ever heard a story of forgiveness like this before.**

Love of Enemies
The hardest people to love are your enemies. As we said in the forgiveness introduction, early prayers were a form of cursing your enemies. In Matthew 5, Jesus continued to talk about forgiveness when he discussed the ideology of an *eye for an eye.* "You have heard that it was said, 'Eye for eye, and tooth for tooth. But I tell you, do not resist an evil person. If anyone slaps you on the right cheek, turn to them the other cheek also. And if anyone wants to sue you and take your shirt, hand over your coat as well.[41] If anyone forces you to go one mile, go with them two miles."

The slap on the right cheek remark causes a lot of confusion. There are times when Jesus talks about self-defense and even having to take up a sword. The reason He says "the right cheek" is because in the Jewish culture of the day, (and in contemporary cultures where sanitary conditions like toilet paper are not available) you would eat and shake hands with your right hand only and you would not touch anyone or anything in public with your left hand. If you were struck on your right cheek, it would have been a backhanded slap of disrespect, not what we would think of as an aggressive punch.

In Luke 22:36, we see an example of a time Jesus did tell His disciples to have a sword. "He said to them, 'But now if you have a purse, take it, and also a bag; and if you don't have a **sword, sell your cloak and buy one.** The disciples said, "See, Lord, here are two **sword**s." "That's enough!" he replied'".

Jesus also explained the unheard-of idea of praying for those who persecute you. In Matthew 5 Jesus tells His disciples, "You have heard that it was said, 'Love your neighbor and hate your enemy.' But I tell you, love your enemies and pray for those who persecute you, that you may be children of your Father in heaven. He causes his sun to rise on the evil and the good and sends rain on the righteous and the unrighteous."

As verse 46 continues, Jesus draws a comparison to how pagans would react, and he is pointing out a different way of reacting.

"If you love those who love you, what reward will you get? .... And if you greet only your own people, what are you doing more than others? Do not even pagans do that? Be perfect, therefore, as your heavenly Father is perfect."

Jesus ends this advice to love those who do not love you because it is what is intended for us by our heavenly father.

Forgiven Sins

Just like redemption, the Christian idea of Forgiveness of Sins is unique. **All other historical thoughts of this concept followed because of the words and ideas of Jesus**. The first step toward understanding the idea of forgiven sins is understanding the concept of forgiveness and forgiving others. The next step is for each person to realize that you can be forgiven by God for all your sins. **This is a uniquely Christian and almost exclusively Christian concept.** The Hindus, the Buddhists, the Muslims, do not have this concept. If your spiritual worldview is one where you believe you are saved by works, a bad deed can only be overridden by more good deeds, not by forgiveness.

The Hindus, Buddhists and Muslims believe you must do more good works than bad works. You are not forgiven for your bad works; you must do more good works to atone for the bad works.

The Judeo-Christian idea that humans are created in the image of God means all humans are worthy of respect and honor, and they are unique and sovereign. This idea was virtually nonexistent at the time Jesus began teaching. Jesus was the first human to exhibit words and actions that proved he believed all humans were worthy of respect and honor. **Jesus was the first human in written history to treat all humans as fully human**.

The True Nature of Love

A deep understanding of the concepts of forgiveness and love goes hand in hand. If you cannot forgive someone, you cannot truly love them, and if you do not have a strong concept of love, it is difficult to forgive others. The teachings of Jesus are an amazing quilt of talks and parables about love of self, love of others, and love of God that are the basis of the Western Culture that has driven all human progress to new heights, especially over the past 100 + years. Most people in The West take these ideas for granted but if you look at cultures that don't have these foundational concepts it is easy to justify social institutions like a caste system and all forms of oppression.

Jesus sets a new standard for what love is. That standard is radically different from the pagan beliefs of his day.

Jesus's new concept of **Loving your Neighbor** (what we currently call **human rights**) and loving people different from you, (what we currently call **diversity**) are discussed in the parable of *the Good Samaritan.* In Luke 10:25, Jesus tells how a successful Samaritan man was on the road from Jerusalem to Jericho which was known as a dangerous road.

The parable begins when a legal expert is trying to trap Jesus when he asks, "what must I do to inherit eternal life?" (which was the same as how do I get to heaven?)

Jesus asks, "What is written in the law?" The lawyer quotes scripture when he says, "Love the Lord your God with all your heart and with all your soul and with all your strength and with all your mind and love your neighbor as yourself." Jesus says, "do this you will live." Then the lawyer asks, "Who is my neighbor?"

In the Hebrew culture of the time, the people who were considered 'neighbors' to Jews were Priests, Levites, and other common Jews. All Jews were responsible to these folks. Samaritans were categorically excluded because they were generally viewed with disdain by the Jews and there was much animosity between the Jews and Samaritans. The parable begins when the robbers stripped and beat a man on the road. First a Priest of Israel saw the man and passed by on the other side of the road. Then a Levite looks at the situation and passes by on the other side of the road. Then a Samaritan who is considered an enemy of the Jewish people, sees the beaten-up man and has compassion for him, so he helps bandage the man's wounds and takes him to an Inn and tells the innkeeper he will cover all the man's expenses.

Jesus then asks the lawyer which of the three men was his neighbor? The Lawyer answered, "the one who had mercy on him." Jesus then tells the Lawyer, "Go and do likewise."

The list of radical new ideas Jesus taught about human rights, love of enemies, our relationship to God, and the unity of the physical and the spiritual world were so totally unique and life changing **they became the foundation of what came to be Western Culture**. No matter what else you believe about Jesus, everyone must acknowledge the tremendous impact He had on the way people view their relationship to God, and to people that are different than themselves.

Chapter 5 Study Questions

Was there a general concept of forgiveness before Jesus?

What was the name of the Hebrew tradition that cast out a family member who associated with people from other cultures?

What is the name of the parable where Jesus first began to radically change the human concept of forgiveness?

What story talks about Jesus's thoughts about Women's Rights?

In what parable did Jesus talk about loving your enemy and caring for people of other cultures?

What story talked about Jesus forgiving a woman caught in adultery?

Chapter 6
Spiritual Consciousness Revolution,
The Holy Spirit and The New Covenant

The discussion of Spiritual Consciousness can lead in many directions and to many places. For those who are serious and go where the spirit leads, my belief is the discussion ultimately progresses to understanding The Holy Spirit. For those who seriously study the words and actions of Jesus, they find He is the first human rights advocate in human history. He was also the first person to discuss what it means to be spiritual, the relationship of God and Man, and the afterlife. For those who continue to understand the teachings of Jesus, they move to understanding the concept of forgiven sins, redemption, and salvation. The hard part most people don't get to, or are confused by, is understanding the Holy Spirit.

As humans progressed from tribal, emotional, and instinct driven individual actions and societies, there had to be a point where humanity as a group began to think about and understand their spiritual nature. The first glimpse of this came in the period of Greek philosophy. For the Hebrews before Jesus the Sadducees did not believe in resurrection but the Pharisees did talk about resurrection. For the most part it was in regard to your soul going to heaven or hell after you die. The mythology of ancient gods did NOT have any clear discussions of life on earth after death. Plato and Aristotle began to talk about "The Soul" but again, no specific thoughts about resurrection, or what the afterlife was all about.

The Resurrection of Jesus was the defining point when humans began to think about and try to understand the concept of human spirituality and life after death. The Christian concept of Resurrection differs from the concept of reincarnation of the Eastern Religions. Christians believe you get one shot at physical life. The Hindus and Buddhists believe you have many lives and many chances to get to

Moksha or enlightenment. The Christian concept is that you only have one chance at a physical body and there is a bodily resurrection where the body you have in the physical life is a new spiritual body that is somewhat similar to the body you had in the physical life. After Jesus was resurrected his many wounds were healed, he ate with his disciples, and he seemed to have the ability to just appear in different places at different times. After the resurrection Jesus's new body did not have the restrictions of space and time that we understand in the natural world today. Obviously, the human mind is going to have a hard time understanding the concept of resurrection. In the previously referenced book, <u>Believing is Seeing</u>, by Michael Guillen, the well-respected scientist gives a layman's explanation for resurrection by saying Einstein proved in his theory $E=mc^2$ that light can become matter and vice versa. He also stated that when matter reaches the speed of light, it becomes timeless. Guillen is a scientist who looked deeply into the Truth and after many years of searching the physical evidence, he found God. His book explains miracles like the resurrection in scientific terms.

Understanding that which is hard to understand.
We are now in the deep waters of human cognitive understanding. The best way our minds handle big concepts is through stories. Stories give us structure to help us understand new concepts.

Archetypes or Actuality
Many people ask, "Is the Bible made up of true stories that actually happened or are they just archetypes of general truths?" We all must answer that for ourselves, but the important thing is to use the stories of the Bible to help us understand that which is hard to understand.

The Bible is without a doubt the greatest, deepest, most well read, and most complete history book ever written. To help us understand the deep concept of The Holy Spirit we will review the Biblical story of Adam and Eve to help us imagine and understand how human life started.

From a Christian viewpoint, when Adam and Eve were in the Garden, they *were spiritually One with God.* Their awareness of God was stronger than their awareness of the physical world or their physical bodies. I think you can make the case that if Adam and Eve would NOT have separated themselves from God's Will their spiritual bodies would have lived forever in the Garden (which was Paradise).

Understanding Sin
The story of Adam and Eve is about humans exercising their Free Will and separating themselves from God's instructions or the Will of God.

Sin = Separation from God = Spiritual Death. If you believe there is a spiritual God who created the world, then it is logical to say everything physical is preceded by something spiritual. Spiritual death had to precede physical death. God told Adam and Eve they could do whatever they wanted, with one exception. There was just one simple rule. Do not eat the fruit of the tree of good and evil. God told Adam if they ate the fruit they would surely die.[2]

The tree of good and evil represented their ability to choose good from evil. Free will is one of the things that separates us from animals. Animals act based on instinct not free will and reason. Adam and Eve eating the forbidden fruit is an illustration that if humans are in paradise and they have everything they would ever need they will always be tempted to separate themselves from the Will of God or the Spirit of God, even under the threat of death. Humans have an instinct towards freedom or self-expression or independence, that takes them outside of the way God ordered the world. It was hard for Adam and Eve to understand God when God was the only other person in their life. To this day it is hard for humans to understand God when we are surrounded by a physical world that is separated from most forms of spiritual understanding.

The Bible tells us, God kicked Adam and Eve out of Paradise because the tree of eternal life was also in the garden and if they would have eaten from the tree of eternal life, they would have lived forever, separated from God. God did not want that. From the time humans separated themselves from God's Will and God's order, God had a plan to reunite them with the original Unity and order He designed.

The significance of eating *the forbidden fruit* is that when you eat something it becomes part of you. If you eat something very harmful, like bad food or drugs, it can disrupt the biology of your body immediately and for future generations. When Adam and Eve disobeyed God, and exercised their Free Will apart from God, it disrupted their spiritual understanding and their spiritual relationship with God for themselves and for future generations. Adam and Eve did not know any shame until they separated themselves from God's Will. Once they did what God told them not to do, they felt shame immediately and they hid from God. The first thing God did when He talked to them after they ate the fruit was to **give them a chance to repent**. **They did not repent,** they blamed each other and the snake for tempting them. They would not admit they disobeyed God's warnings when God confronted them. For God to reinstate the spiritual relationship with humans it would take an act of **Divine Repentance and Divine Justice**. God had to be sure humans had progressed intellectually if not spiritually, enough to grasp what was going on before He made the next move.

An important spiritual concept is that ***God does not violate our Free Will***. God allows humans to do evil when they choose. When we step outside of God's Will or God's order, we remove ourselves from the shadow of God's blessing. As individuals and as nations, when we remove ourselves from God's Will, God leaves us to our own devices, until we get ourselves back in God's Will, or God's order.

The story of Adam and Eve tells us that humans were once spiritually One with God and due to the Sin of going against God's instructions or God's Will, humans fell out of that divine relationship. In the beginning, humans were God-Centered, NOT Self-Centered. They were spiritually aligned with God. Before Adam and Eve separated themselves from God's Will it says they were naked and not ashamed. Once they separated themselves from God, it says they realized they were naked, which was a heightened awareness of the physical world, and they hid from God. When we are following God's Will we are concerned about the spiritual world, or spiritual laws, or God's laws and doing what is right in God's eyes. When we separate from God, we become caught up in the physical world and we begin to feel shame and worry about our physical bodies and how we appear to others. When you separate yourself from God's Divine Will you begin seeing the world and yourself through your own selfish eyes and not with the eyes of God you were born with. You are understanding the world from a selfish physical or material perspective and not from a spiritual, or God's, perspective. We are not ashamed of anything or physical appearances when we are centered on God. When we become centered on ourselves and not God, we become worried and possibly ashamed of what will we wear or what we will eat or other physical things.

The story of Adam and Eve says humans were spiritually One with God, they fell out of that relationship by exerting their Free Will apart from God's Will. For humans to get back in the right relationship with God the scales of Divine Justice had to be balanced. The Bible tells the story of human history from Adam to Jesus which is the story of God trying to get humanity back in the right relationship to God. The Bible says Jesus was the person who came to pay the Divine Sacrifice, the Divine price, to get humans back in the right relationship with God. Jesus' actions of being willing to die sacrificially balanced the scale for an unrepentant mankind to that point. Redeeming mankind is one of the many levels of meaning to the life of Jesus.

The secular world does NOT believe humans were ever spiritually connected to God, so there is no need for humans to be redeemed or reunited with God. For the secular world I would say Jesus was the first human to talk about *the spiritual nature of humanity.*

One last mention of **The Holy Spirit.** From the time of Adam to the time of Jesus, the Holy Spirit or the Spirit of God would only appear at specific times for a specific purpose. Jesus came to humanity and redeemed or reunited humans to God.

He balanced the scales of Divine Justice. Once Jesus left the earth, The Holy Spirit would be available to all people all the time because of the final sacrifice of Jesus. After Jesus left the earth, The Holy Spirit (which is part of The Trinity) was available for everyone. Just like God leaves you to your own devices if you separate from Him, The Holy Spirit will only come into your life if you want Him in your life.

The Holy Spirit is a difficult concept. Jeremiah and Isaiah prophesied the coming of the Holy Spirit. God said He would put the law in their minds and write it in their hearts. In Jeremiah 31:31 The Lord says, "'The days are coming', declares the Lord, 'when I will make a new covenant with the people of Israel and with the people of Judah. 32 It will not be like the covenant I made with their ancestors when I took them by the hand to lead them out of Egypt, because they broke my covenant, though I was a husband to them," declares the Lord. "This is the covenant I will make with the people of Israel after that time, declares the Lord. "I will put my law in their minds and write it on their hearts. I will be their God, and they will be my people. No longer will they teach their neighbor, or say to one another, know the Lord, because they will all know me, from the least of them to the greatest," declares the Lord. "For I will forgive their wickedness and will remember their sins no more.'"

Jesus's life was the transition point between the Old and New Testaments and the original Covenants between God and Mankind, and The New Covenant. In a Last Will and Testament for the Testament to go into effect the testator must die. Jesus came to redeem the broken relation between God and Humanity and to educate humans about their spiritual nature and what to expect from the Holy Spirit in the New Covenant. Jesus talked a lot about the Holy Spirit and in John 20:21, He told His disciples, "Again Jesus said, "Peace be with you! As the Father has sent me, I am sending you." And with that he breathed on them and said, "Receive the Holy Spirit.'"

Christianity is the only Spiritual Worldview that has a concept of The Holy Spirit. Ultimately it is the idea that there is a spiritual realm in which we are all connected with God and just as you tune a radio to accept a certain frequency, or you find a Wi-Fi connection for your phone or computer, we all have that ability to tune into God and we must develop that ability to be able to find and tune into God's streaming service. Think of it as being united with God in a Group Chat that never ends unless you disconnect.

The New Covenant
God's Covenants with mankind were unconditional promises God made to humans. The history of humans to the time of Jesus is a history of humans struggling to understand and live according to God's order and rules. Jesus ushered in the last phase of spiritual consciousness development, which is the spiritual age. Jesus came to teach about, and then demonstrate, that humans are spiritual in nature, and we are spirits that live in a body and our actions should be motivated by spiritual laws, not instinct, emotions, intellect, or reason. The Old Testament of the Bible was simply God trying to teach people to live by the laws of God, not the laws of men. One of the many things

Jesus did in The New Covenant or the New Testament, was to explain the spiritual nature of humanity and the spiritual meaning behind God's laws. **Jesus was stepping up the spiritual consciousness development of humanity from a simply physical understanding to a spiritual understanding of reality.**

Jesus said, "if your right eye causes you to stumble, gouge it out and throw it away, … if your right hand causes you to stumble cut it off and throw it away."[3] Jesus said committing adultery in your heart is as bad as actually committing physical adultery. This is the new idea, **that your heart, or your spirit, should be what motivates you and not your physical wants and needs**. The heart symbolizes what is at the center of your being, which is your spirit. Jesus definitely raised the bar of expectations of moral actions for all of humanity!

The Spiritual Revolution
The Hebrew society had very little understanding of spirituality or the true nature of the spiritual world when Jesus began preaching. All anyone understood was the physical world was ruled by physical force. They thought the Messiah would be a powerful warrior who would overturn the Roman government by physical force. That was the only way a government or society had ever been changed up until that time. The idea of a spiritual revolution was something that took years and generations for humans to understand. Before Jesus, one Rabbi would go into the Holy of Holies and talk to God once a year. The other Rabbis were not sure what would happen so they tied a rope around him in case he was struck dead, and they had to pull him out because no one else could enter that room. At Pentecost when the Holy Spirit was released throughout all humanity, instantly all humans had spiritual access to God. I cannot overstate the difference between a relationship with God based on laws, and a relationship when His understanding is written on everyone's heart or in their spirit. **The change**

in how humanity comes to know God is what the Bible is all about.

The difficulty of understanding the laws of God is best portrayed in Matthew 16:21 when near the end of Jesus's earthly ministry, he told the disciples "He must go to Jerusalem and suffer many things at the hands of the elders, the chief priests and the teachers of the law, and that he must be killed and on the third day be raised to life." Peter had no clue what Jesus was saying and in verse 22 he said, "Never, Lord! This shall never happen to you!" Jesus rebuked Peter in verse 23 when He said, "Get behind me, Satan! You are a stumbling block to me; you do not have in mind the concerns of God, but merely human concerns."

The resurrection of Jesus fundamentally changed the debate about spirituality for all human history. When Peter, Paul, and the other disciples began preaching *Christ crucified,* it was a fundamental shift in the way humans perceived their own existence. The story of the Coming Messiah was prophesied for thousands of years, and then a human was born who was the Unity of Divinity and Humanity, the spiritual and the physical. Jesus performed every kind of miracle imaginable to prove the spiritual world precedes and affects the physical world. While He was alive, He performed many miracles to prove He had total command of all the forces of nature. It was hard for people to understand and believe, but when He was resurrected from an agonizing and grueling physical death experience it helped convinced people there is a power that transcends reality or the physical world as we know it.

For those who believe in a Creator we must believe that a created being can never fully understand the One who created us. The Trinity is the best way to try to describe God, but we must realize that God exists beyond space and time, **so trying to understand God in *rational terms* is not possible.**

The Trinity

The best way I can describe God is pure, intense energy, exponentially more powerful than the sun or a nuclear bomb, or anything you can understand or imagine. Think of God as the energy source that powers the sun and all of humanity. If anyone *sees* God, they burn up because He is pure, intense, self-sustaining energy. The burning bush is a way to describe energy that does not burn up, dissipate, or go away. Jesus is the form of God that humans can see and understand. When God wants to appear to humans, He appears in the form of Jesus. Jesus is *the transformer* that powers down the intense energy of God's Presence so humans can get close to God. The Holy Spirit is like God's internet that allows him to communicate with everyone that dials him up.

Paul was one of the first to write about this new understanding of the relationship between the physical to the spiritual body.

In I Corinthians 15:46, Paul says, "the spiritual did not come first, but the natural, and **after that the spiritual.**"

The context is as follows: it is sown a natural body; it is raised a spiritual body. If there is a natural body, there is also a spiritual body. So it is written: "The first man Adam became a living being, **the last Adam (Jesus), a life-giving spirit**. The spiritual did not come first, but the natural, and after that the spiritual. The first man was of the dust of the earth; the second man is of heaven. And just as we have borne the image of the earthly man, so shall we bear the image of the heavenly man." This is Paul's way of initially describing the *Paradox of Human Existence*, that we come to realize we are spiritual in nature through a natural body and mind.

The following is an account of how difficult it was for many followers of Jesus to understand what He was talking about when He spoke of the resurrection and that He was the Bread of Life. John 6:60 says, "on hearing it, many of his disciples said, "This is a hard teaching. Who can accept it?"

[61] Aware that his disciples were grumbling about this, Jesus said to them, "Does this offend you? Then what if you see the Son of Man ascend to where he was before! [63] The Spirit gives life; the flesh counts for nothing. The words I have spoken to you—*they are full of the Spirit and life.*" … **From this time many of his disciples turned back and no longer followed him.""**

As Paul traveled between Jerusalem and Rome preaching the gospel, one of his main topics was *Christ crucified.* The resurrection of Christ was physical evidence to all of humanity that the Spirit survives the body and that there is a spiritual dimension to human existence.

When God finally released His Spirit upon the world it began the **FINAL PHASE OF THE SPIRITUAL DEVELOPMENT OF HUMANITY.**

Genesis 3 tells us that humans let our spiritual relation with God die which caused us to die physically. To get back in the right relation to God we need to learn to die to the physical world and the world of Sin (which is separation from God) to come back to life with the Spirit of God.

Jesus said He was God incarnate and He came to *heal* all people, not just the Jews, from all forms of suffering. He did this by appealing to God's Will. He came to demonstrate how to liberate the physical ego and spirit from its physical body so humans could take the next step toward spiritual development or spiritual life.

It was hard for folks from the Abrahamic days to follow God's simple Laws of the Ten Commandments. Now God was giving them something even more difficult to understand. The new concept was that humans are truly spiritual in nature and the New Covenant was a covenant of Love and the Spirit and not simply about following laws. Under the New Covenant you followed God's Will because you love Him. People in Moses' time would not have been able to understand this. Certainly, God had to come back to earth to explain it. God had a do over!

In summary, I would contend that all humans are spiritually related to God. When humans began to exercise their free will apart from God, they became spiritually dead, and they eventually became total physical beings with little or no sense of spirituality. The mission of Jesus was to redeem humans to God by sacrificing His life as the final sacrifice to God to pay the price for all human sins and to prove to humans that the spiritual world precedes and transcends the physical world. The point is, ultimately, we all must die to the physical world to live spiritually, but if we learn to live spiritually in the physical world our spirits will survive physical death.

Chapter 6 Study Questions

Name two prophets who talked about the Holy Spirit.

What is the significance of Adam and Eve eating the forbidden fruit?

Does God violate our Free Will?

What is the author's definition of Sin? (capital S)

What action changed the debate about spirituality and the afterlife?

Was The New Covenant about Laws?

Chapter 7
The Rise of the Church

The Church is often called *The Body of Christ*. Those who believe in the Resurrection become the hands and feet and heart of Jesus in the physical world. For the first three centuries after the time of Christ, Christians and the Christian Church were persecuted in varying degrees. Some historians agree that when Rome burned, Nero blamed it on the Christians who, he said, were worshiping the wrong god. Nero used that as an excuse to have Peter and Paul executed.[1]

In areas of less persecution, the Church developed a system to elect bishops by 200 AD.[2]

Before Emperor Constantine came to power in 306 AD., Rome went through a period of seventy-five years of civil wars and internal strife as various Emperors battled for control of the empire. The story goes that each general would pick a god to worship and many times they believed the result of the battle was based on whose god was more powerful. Constantine decided to solicit the help of the Christian God. Constantine's men painted crosses on their shields. They won several battles. Due to the victories, Constantine consolidated power, united the Roman Empire, and ended the persecution of Christians in 313 AD. The edict of Milan of 313 declared tolerance for Christians in the Roman Empire and the Christian Church became a recognized institution. Many people began to practice many forms of Christian worship. In 325 AD, Constantine formed the council of Nicaea, which tried to formalize and standardize the Christian religion. The council produced the Nicaean Creed. Wikipedia says, The age of Constantine marks a distinct epoch in the history of the Roman Empire and a pivotal moment in the transition from classical antiquity to the Middle Ages.[3]

One of the results of the Nicaean Council meeting was they decided that Bishops would be elected. The Christian Church, which became very powerful, was one of the first major institution where the rulers were elected. The Christian church had a *Universal appeal.* The world was made up of many cultures with many gods. As Paul, the disciples and others spread to the ends of the earth, their message cut across all cultures. The teachings of Jesus were radically different than anything anyone had ever heard before. Over the next thousand years the Roman empire and the Catholic church rose in power and dominance and, of course, became corrupt.

The church and the Roman Empire grew together
On Christmas Day 800, Pope Leo III crowned Charlemagne Emperor of the Holy Roman Empire, forming the political and religious foundations of Christendom and establishing in earnest the French government's longstanding historical association with the Roman Catholic Church.

By the 1500s, the Church became many things to many people throughout the world, but the Catholic Church backed by Rome was what many people thought of as The Church. In 1517 Martin Luther started the reformation when he published his 97 treatises which were his objections to what he believed were the corrupt practices of the Catholic Church. One of the main forms of income for the corrupted local churches was *selling penances.* If a person sinned you were forgiven when you gave money, or crops, or livestock, to the church. Luther took exception to this practice. Luther's main idea was that you do not gain forgiveness for sins by paying a penance to the Church or anyone else, you can only gain forgiveness through the Grace of God, and you are saved by faith not works or alms.

The Reformation brought forth the ideas that you are defined by your own thoughts and not by the traditions of your culture, the church, or other institutions. When a single German Monk took on the Catholic Church it shook the

70

world that one man could take on and change one of the world's largest and most powerful institutions. Luther was considered a protester and his movement began what became The Protestant and Orthodox Churches.

The Magna Carta was written in 1200. It gained an upsurge of interest in the late 1500s as the Reformation took hold. The main idea that was taken from the Magna Carta was, **all people are Equal Under the Law** and individual freedom should not be subject to the arbitrary whims of a king. It took a while for common people to understand this new idea and it took even longer for the Monarchs and other rulers to give up their arbitrary power that was based on force or tradition.

The Church of England splits with Rome
King Henry VIII's desire to have a male heir is well known and was the impetus behind his many wives and some of their untimely demises. A letter sent by Henry and his court to Pope Clement VII in 1530 asked for the annulment of his first marriage to Catherine of Aragon. The king wished to move on to a new, younger bride who might be able to deliver on his quest for a son. This letter was the opening salvo of a battle between Henry and Clement that resulted in the English church breaking from the Catholic church and going its own way. In effect, the entire nation of England was at least in part driven to re-position itself against Rome to satisfy the personal desires of its King.

Although Henry ultimately wanted an heir, the issue of finances may also have been a significant factor in the split between the Catholic church and Great Britain. The Catholic Church held many profitable lands and operated hundreds of monasteries throughout the British Isles. When Henry decided to break off and form his own church, all Catholic lands were confiscated, and the monastery inhabitants were sent packing. Everything was confiscated by the crown and Henry quickly found new riches and powers he did not have before. Although it may not have been the primary reason for the separation, money probably did play a major role.

Although Henry VIII had the ultimate power to make a break with the church, the people of Britain largely aligned with Protestant beliefs and as such, complied with an overall reformation of the church. The existing separation was based on both geography and belief. With no more allegiance to the Pope and the teachings of the Roman Catholic tradition, English Protestants returned to the Bible as the basis for their religion. The break that began under Henry was not complete until Elizabeth I again broke with Rome in 1558 after Mary Tudor's brief realignment in 1555.[4]

It was the belief of British subjects and the king himself that the monarch was the representative of God on earth. Today the sitting ruler is still the "defender of the faith" and true leader of the Church of England. Unlike the United States where there is a clear separation of church and state, British law joins the two as a result of the split that occurred in the 16th century. In Britain the Monarch is both the head of state and the head of the church. This means the kingdom is Anglican by definition.

Whether you call it The Reformation, The Enlightenment, or The Age of Reason, what was happening was *The Western World* was going through a big transition of individual and social consciousness development. The Western World was transitioning from the tribal emotional and traditional stage to the *second stage*, where the society is organized by reason and ideology. Those who were truly motivated by the Christian Gospel were making the transition to the third stage which was the Spiritual stage of individual and social human consciousness development.

Chapter 7 Study Questions

What are the three stages of human social development?

What Roman Emperor ended the persecution of Christians?

What was the first attempt to standardize the Christian Religion?

What was one of the main complaints of Martin Luther's 97 treatises that helped start the Reformation?

Chapter 8
Understanding America's Roots

Christopher Columbus was a very Christian man. He was born in Italy and he always loved the craft of sailing. His writings are evidence that he was a great sailor and explorer who was *moved by The Holy Spirit* to find new lands and spread the Gospel to the ends of the earth. Columbus spent seven years before 1492 contacting the major Monarchs in Europe trying to find one person or government that would back his efforts. After seven years Queen Isabella of Spain agreed to fund the explorations of Columbus. His diary says, "It was the Lord who put into my mind (I could feel his hand upon me) the fact that it would be possible to sail from here to the Indies. All who heard of my project rejected it with laughter, ridiculing me. **There is no question that the inspiration was from the Holy Spirit**, because He comforted me with rays of marvelous inspiration from the Holy Scriptures."[1]

The discovery of America opened a new vision of freedom for the people of Western Europe. In 1620, 110 Puritans from England, described as adventurers, tradesmen, and servants, decided to leave the religious oppression of King James of England, and seek out the freedom of the New World. They were backed by the Virginia Company, who had previously sent out three ships carrying 105 passengers who founded Jamestown in 1607.[2] When the pilgrims landed in what is now Massachusetts, they realized they were not under the authority of the King of England, and since they were not in Virginia they were not under the jurisdiction of The Virginia Company. They put together the **Mayflower Compact which was the first time a community of equal people organized a government by means of a social contract that stated the government would rule by consent of the governed.**[3] This was the beginning of Democracy with a strong Christian foundation.

What was remarkable about this particular contract was that it was not between a servant and a master or a people and a king, but between a group of like-minded individuals with God as a witness and symbolic co- signatory. [4]

As all of this was happening in America. In England, Charles I, took over after James, who became more oppressive, and more Puritans realized the only way to find a community where Christians could live in freedom and practice their religion was to leave England for the New World. The Bible had recently been translated into English and for the first-time common people could read the scriptures and try to understand the true meaning of the Gospels and not just rely on the version the clergy or governments were using to try and control the masses.

The Mayflower Compact predated John Locke's famous *Second Treatise of Government* which seventy years later made famous the idea that "All people deserve equal protection under the law and the role of government is to protect individual freedom, and life, liberty and property".[5]

Peter Marshall, in his book <u>The Light and the Glory</u>, notes that the Pilgrims believed, "That the Kingdom of God could be built on earth in their lifetimes... They knew that they were sinners. But like the religious pilgrims before them, they were dedicated to actually living together in obedience to God's laws under the Lordship of Jesus Christ."[6]

America was founded as a Christian Nation **based on the laws of God.** Early Pilgrims referred to America as The New Israel and The Promised land.[7] As North America developed, the people eventually realized they would need to make a complete split from England. They began studying everything they could find about how to organize a society in the right way according to the rules of God.

The founding of the United States of America took a culture from the era of Kings directly to a government based on

Spiritual Laws, or the Laws of The God of The Bible. **This was the first time since Moses and only the second time in human history that a government was organized based on spiritual laws or the laws of God, NOT the laws of men.**

The Great Awakening in America
In his book Persecution, David Limbaugh points out that many people believed the American Revolution was as much if not more influenced by the French Enlightenment thinking as it was influenced by Christianity. He cites many references to show between 1730 and the Revolution America truly found itself spiritually during this period, honing its unique cultural identity centered on Christian principles and "inalienable rights" which were a product of biblical theism.[8]

Not since the time of Moses had a group of individuals tried to truly organize a society based on the Laws of God or Spiritual Laws.

The Declaration of Independence
Some historians have said the American Founders were not really Christians and they looked to the Romans and The Greeks more than scriptures. The book, Persecution, also refutes the idea that Jefferson and crew were influenced by the Greeks or Romans more than Christian scripture. The following is a quote from historian Gary Amos: "The French scholar Michel Villey, himself a humanist, and other scholars, such as Richard Tuck of England, have shown that Greek and Roman ideas concerning "rights" did not form the philosophical underpinnings of the American (or English) system as secularists insist.

Amos explained that the concept of inalienable rights couldn't have come from the Greeks or Romans but is traceable to the Scriptures (of The Bible). The Greeks, said Amos, were polytheists who would never have subscribed to the notion that all people are created equal and are endowed by their Creator (singular) with certain unalienable rights.[9] Moreover, according to Amos, the Greeks believed the universe originated from an impersonal divine force, not a personal God as revealed in the Bible. Human beings were an extension of the divine force; there was virtually no distinction between humans and the divine, so the Declaration's concept of men being endowed by their Creator would never have occurred to the Greeks. Only in the Bible are the components of the Declaration's phrase, "all men are created equal and endowed by their Creator (singular) with certain unalienable rights" present. It is a Biblical concept that God created man in His Image and Likeness. Only because of this are all men entitled to equal treatment and inalienable rights. The Greeks did not subscribe to a doctrine of equality or equal rights. Neither did the Romans. Had Thomas Jefferson decided to do so, he could have endorsed secularism in his draft of the Declaration, but instead chose language compatible with a biblical worldview."[10]

When America was founded, it was solidly a Judeo-Christian Nation.

Chapter 8 Study Questions

What drove Christopher Columbus to believe he would find a new world West of Europe?

What was unique about the Mayflower Compact?

Why did the phrase *endowed by their creator with certain inalienable rights* have to come from the Biblical worldview?

Chapter 9
A Step Backward
Darwinism and Existentialism

As the Age of Reason and the Enlightenment blossomed in Europe, the secular movement followed. I mentioned earlier that there are three major phases of human development. In an agrarian society, it is easier to get from phase one or two to phase three which is the spiritual phase. When you grow your own food, and whether you eat or not depends on how well you plant the seeds and if you get the proper amount of sun and rain, you feel a much stronger connection to Nature and to Nature's God. When your house, and your furniture, is made from the trees you, or someone you know cut down and chopped up, you understand the close dependence humans have on nature. As the world becomes industrialized and modernized and humans end up living in concrete jungles with no idea where the materials they use, or the food they eat comes from, they no longer understand how dependent or connected we still are to nature and each other. Over the course of time humans realized how to turn sand into glass which first became small windows and then walls for huge commercial buildings, and eventually fiber optics and microchips. We learned how to use petroleum to power machines that multiplied human productivity by a factor of hundreds. Then we learned how to turn petroleum into plastics.

As *The Age of Reason* matured, humans mastered the incredible natural resources of the earth. Instead of appreciating our dependence on them, we began to take them for granted.

Once the connection with an appreciation of nature was lost, the ability to understand our spiritual nature became more difficult. As humans mastered and became comfortable in the industrialized, material world, the need to understand the spiritual dimension seemed non-existent or unnecessary.

The century from 1770 to 1870 was an incredible time for the USA. America was at war much of the time. With England, then France, then Spain, with the indigenous people, and eventually with itself. From the late 1800s to the end of the twentieth century, Christian thinking began to wane in America and throughout the Western World. We will do a quick review of a good book that traces the history of the change from a strong Christian ideological basis to a more Existentialist worldview for a growing part of the world from the 1600's to the present.

In his book <u>The Universe Next Door</u>, James W. Sire traces the development of organized existentialist or non-religious and non-spiritual thinking. The following is a basic outline of ideas from Sire's book. This is a very insightful book, and it illustrates how much the Western worldview has moved from a spiritual to a non-spiritual worldview.

By tracing the steps of *Western* cultural thinking from Christianity to Existentialism over several hundred years we will get a feel for the major principles of these ideas.

In the 1600's the basic principles of Christianity were as follows:

- God is a spirit being who created the world.

- God has a personality. **We can know God**. We can know the world around us.

- God "communicates" with us **through *Revealed Knowledge* using the scripture of the Bible   and through prayer.**

- There is a **Triune God**–God the Father, Jesus the Son, and The Holy Ghost.

- God physically **appeared to humanity in the form of Jesus** to help humanity understand the spiritual side of reality and our relationship to God. More importantly, He came to Redeem all sinners.

- Morality, Good and Evil, **Right and Wrong, are based on the revealed knowledge of Scripture**, which is **God's Word made known to humanity**. [1]

Above are some of the basic principles of Christianity. Sire's book then recaps the subtle changes that moved cultural thought away from Christianity to Deism and on to existentialism. The shift started in the 17th century during the Age of Reason. The first step was a change in how we know God. Traditional Christianity believes you know God through understanding Scripture and through prayer. The first change in the Age of Reason is the belief that you can understand God through REASON. The first shift away from Christian thought is that spiritual knowledge comes through your own experience, not revelation or revealed or innate knowledge. The first step away from Christian thought is that you must use your reason to interpret scripture or to understand spirituality in your own way.

In the 1600's Western culture was beginning to use Reason to interpret experience. This period ushered in the birth of science and the "age of reason" as man began to learn more and more about the world around him through science and reason. Peter Medawar agrees with this: "The 17th Century doctrine of *the necessity of reason* was slowly giving way to the belief in the *sufficiency* of reason".[2] This statement means you can know everything you need to know about the world merely by using your own reason. People began to believe that you understand God through your own reason, NOT through revealed knowledge. People began to believe that ALL knowledge, including knowledge about God, comes through human reason not through scripture or *revealed knowledge*.

It was a major paradigm shift when people began to interpret God and scripture through reason and science, instead of interpreting reality through scripture. Sire points out that ideas about God changed in the age of reason. People began to believe that God created the Universe but is NOT involved anymore. God merely set things in motion. They began to think God is NOT a PERSONAL God–he is a Dis-Interested Creator.

As people's thoughts about God changed, their thoughts about morality also changed. They began to believe that morality should be based on reason. Morality is what is reasonable not what is scriptural or revealed by God. This gave rise to the belief that there are no absolute or transcendent laws.

Sire says "The god who was discovered by the deists was an architect, but not a lover or a judge or personal in any way".[3] The deists believe God started the world and then became dis-interested. Once revealed knowledge is out of the picture it becomes difficult for the average person to understand how someone could have enough intelligence or experience to see the whole picture and therefore know what is right or wrong. Without an all knowing and all caring God who can communicate what is right and wrong, morality becomes a product of human reason and is subject to many different interpretations and feelings. The next big step was when naturalism began to replace reason.

In chapter four Sire points out that the next shift in the road from Pure Christianity to Existentialism is when naturalism or science replaces reason. All history then becomes merely Science History. That is to say that the only meaning to History is what we make of it. **Science replaces reason, which replaced revelation.** We use science to understand reality, not scripture or reason. History becomes nothing more than Cause and Effect. The Cosmos is all there is. It is just matter that is changing in form. There is no overreaching transcendent purpose. Man's cognitive ability separates him from animals. Moral thought differentiates between "Self-Conscious Beings" and non-self-conscious beings. Moral Thought is based on "Social Harmony" and only related to humans. All history becomes science history.

Self-Consciousness and Self Determination become the highest values.
Naturalism started with Rene Descartes in the mid-1600s, and John Locke's ideas developed into the mid-1700s. Sire says "naturalism had great staying power. Born in the eighteenth century, it came of age in the nineteenth and grew to maturity in the twentieth century".[4] Many naturalists such as Carl Sagan were popular in the late twentieth century. Naturalism was especially strong before the age of supercomputers. Naturalism did well in the age when people thought science could one day explain all existence. An amazing twist began to take place in the twenty-first century. As science progressed, many scientists began to realize the true complexity of the universe and super computers began to calculate that the universe was far too complex, finely tuned and perfectly balanced to have happened by mere chance. Many of the thoughts of people today are based around the concept of global climate change and concern for nature or the environment above all else. This is the ultimate extension of the philosophy of naturalism. When climate change becomes one of the main concerns of the Western World's political leaders this is the sign that naturalism has replaced reason which replaced scripture as the primary worldview.

The final step in the transition from a Christian worldview to pure existentialism was provided by the Nihilists. Some people call Nihilism a worldview. Sire calls it "a denial of all worldviews." [5]

By the 1900s, scripture had been negated and reason had been elevated. By the mid-1900s reason was also negated and science was elevated. Science is the study of mere matter. All that is important is the cause and effect of natural processes. Nihilism then came along and negated Science.

Nihilism negates everything. It negates all purpose, all value, all meaning. Nihilism is the Denial of Philosophy or Religion. It is the denial of the possibility of all knowledge. It also is the denial of all values. First you deny scripture, then you deny reason, then you deny science, then you decide you cannot really know anything.

Existentialism

During the mid-1950's Friedrich Nietzsche, Albert Camus, and Jean Paul Sartre tried to *transcend Nihilism*. Their philosophy was we exist, period.

An existentialist believes that all meaning comes from mere existence. There is no essence. There is nothing essential other than the physical. There is nothing that precedes or transcends existence. There is nothing other than physical existence. All there is, is the physical world, nothing else.

Matter, Time, Chance is all there is

In summary, the quotes and references from Sire above explain how modern Existentialism has evolved from the traditional European and American Christian thought over 400 years. **The intellectual or psychological, or "logical", steps the culture went through to get from Christian theism to existentialism are steps many individual people go through in their own intellectual development.** The big question is how do you act once you become an existentialist? What happens when there is no transcendent God or set of objective values or rules? Meaning becomes every person for themselves and there are no absolutes. Let's discuss what happened when Existentialist philosophy was practiced in recent history.

The Consequences of Existential thought

There are four basic aspects to any world view: origin, meaning, morality and future.

Once an individual or a society has rejected all aspects of a spiritual or a transcendent existence one must then produce a basis for morality and social structure. In most cultures, the meaning, morality, or social structure are related to one's thoughts on essential nature and purpose. If we believe we have no essence and we are just positive and negative electrons brought together by chance, it becomes difficult to put together a code of morality to distinguish right from wrong. In a world where there are no overriding rules, no absolutes, **each person's life becomes a simple matter of avoiding pain and increasing pleasure**. In a world that is not based on a transcendent God, it becomes **everyone for themselves.** You live by your own morals, and I will live by my own morals. If I can do my own thing and express myself, I am good. **Self-centered happiness becomes the greatest virtue.**

Existentialists of the 1800s began the first culture in human civilization that had to deal with the basics of a worldview that was not based on some sort of spiritual or transcendent component of human existence. The result is a culture that struggles to have rules that everyone can agree on. When there are no absolutes that everyone agrees to, it becomes every person for themself and in many cases the strongest, most brutish dictators end up ruling the nation. Society becomes primal again.

Two of the most prominent thinkers of the Existentialist movement were Jean Paul Sartre and Friedrich Nietzsche. Their impact of moral neutrality was a paradigm shift. (Moral neutrality means the culture has no morality, everyone has their own opinion of morality, and everyone's morals are equal).

Many recent historians and observers are beginning to agree that Sartre became the academic godfather to many terrorist movements on the forefront of oppressive nations in the 1960's.

Historian Paul Johnson said of Sartre: "By helping Fanon to inflame Africa, he contributed to the civil wars and mass murders that have engulfed most of that continent from the mid-sixties onward to this day. His influence in Southeast Asia, where the Vietnam War was drawing to a close, was even more baneful. The hideous crimes committed in Cambodia from April 1976 onwards, which involved the deaths of between a fifth and a third of the population were organized by a group of Francophone middle-class intellectuals known as Angka Leu. Of its eight leaders, five were teachers, one a university professor, one a civil servant, and one an economist. All had studied in France in the 1950's where they had not only belonged to the Communist Party but had absorbed Sartre's doctrines of philosophical activism and necessary violence. These mass murderers were his ideological children.[6]

Sartre's impact on people of the 1960's is small compared to Nietzsche's influence on Adolf Hitler. Hitler took Nietzsche's writings as his philosophical blueprint and provoked the bloodiest, most unnecessary, most disruptive war in history, changing irremediably the pattern of the world. Nietzsche's influence on Hitler is undeniable.
Historian William Shirer has written that "Hitler often visited the Nietzsche Museum in Weimar and publicized his veneration for the philosopher by posing for photographs of himself staring in rapture at the bust of the great man"[7] At its height the Hitler regime under Rudolph Hess killed 12,000 people a day at Auschwitz.

In Auschwitz the words of Hitler are clearly stated: I freed Germany from the stupid and degrading fallacies of conscience and morality ... We will train young people before whom the world will tremble. I want young people capable of violence–imperious, relentless, and cruel. Hitler took the metaphysic of Darwinian theory, and in his <u>Mein Kampf</u> said: If nature does not wish that weaker individuals should mate with stronger, she wishes even less that superior race (like the Germanic race) should intermingle with an inferior (like the Jewish race). Why? Because in such a case her efforts, throughout hundreds and thousands of years, to establish an evolutionary higher stage of being, may thus be rendered futile."[8]

It is obvious that the influence of the existentialist thinkers in the mid-20th century was quite substantial and led to a great deal of death and destruction.

The problem of the existentialists is that once any thoughts about a transcendent spirituality disappears it becomes difficult to establish a foundation for morality or meaning. Bertrand Russell, one of the most well-known atheists of the 20th century, admitted he couldn't live as though ethical values were simply a matter of personal taste and that he therefore found his own views 'incredible.' 'I do not know the solution,' he said'.[9]

This quote from Russell illustrates that one of the most well-known atheist existentialists of all times **said moral judgment comes down to feelings**. In a world where you act simply by your feelings there really are no laws.

Another example of the confusion atheists feel is expressed in the following quote, "When you assert that there is such a thing as evil, you must assume there is such a thing as good. When you say there is such a thing as good, you must assume there is a moral law by which to distinguish between good and evil. There must be some standard by which to determine what is good and what is evil. **When you assume a moral law, you must posit a moral lawgiver — the source of the moral law. This moral lawgiver is precisely who atheists are trying to disprove."[10]**

History tells us that when there are no objective or transcendent rules, no morals and no concern for a higher good, bad things happen.

When everyone is only worried about their own self-pleasure then the distinctions between good and evil, and right and wrong disappear, then the culture becomes a free for all.

When Nietzsche said, "God is dead, and we have killed him" he predicted it would lead to a calamity and that is exactly what happened.[11]

I would contend that where the deists, naturalists, and existentialists went wrong is they tried to understand God with human reason. For the Existentialist, reason replaced God and reason was replaced by science or naturalism. Today science has come full circle. Modern scientists, DNA experts, and mathematicians with super computers have realized the Universe we live in is too complex, finely tuned and perfectly balanced to have happened by chance. The only explanation is the explanation more and more scientists are agreeing with, and that is there must be a dimension of reality that is **beyond our reason**. The same "Science" that started people thinking there may not be a God is the science that helped us progress to the point where we realize there has to be a **trans-rational or trans-logical** or spiritual dimension to our existence that transcends reason.[12]

We discussed that there are three stages of human development:

Phase One: the primal, tribal stage where humans are not much different from animals. Their actions are driven by instincts, emotions and tradition, or repetition.

Phase Two: the intellectual, reason or mind stage. It is the stage where the human mind develops the ability to exercise its own free will, and the ego becomes a self-aware I.

Phase Three: the final stage where humans realize their spiritual nature and that their spiritual self transcends the

90

physical world. It is the stage where you realize and actualize your spiritual connection to God and the spiritual world.

A very simple view of what happened with Existentialist thinkers is that they went from Phase Two back to Phase One. Rather than using their minds to understand their spiritual nature they outsmarted themselves and reverted to using feelings, or instincts and emotions as their moral guide for their actions. Reason should lead us to a spiritual understanding that goes beyond reason, it should not lead us back to a hedonistic pleasure over pain morality.

Chapter 9 Study Questions

Do you, or does anyone you know, have a worldview that says everything is just a result of time, matter, and chance?

What were the basic principles of Christian thought in the 1600's?

What ideas changed when Science and Reason replaced the Christian Worldview?

What are some of the key ideas of Naturalism?

What ideas changed to move people from Naturalism to Existentialism?

What are some of the consequences of Existential thought?

Can you have a moral law based on Existentialism?

Give historical examples of what happens when political leaders adopt an existential worldview.

Chapter 10
What is your Worldview?

We have traced the history of the spiritual consciousness development of humans from primal to intellectual to spiritual consciousness. Before we close, we need to discuss Worldviews.

What you think about all of this comes down to your personal worldview. As your mind and your self-aware ego develops its sense of self, the structure it builds to understand everything is a ***personal worldview***.

Your worldview, or your concept of Spirituality, or God, or your spiritual nature, permeates your thinking process your entire life. For most people, it is like running an operating system on their computer. Your computer will not work without an operating system, but until it crashes or has a problem of some sort, most folks don't bother to think about it. **Your thoughts about spirituality or God are the operating software that serve as the foundation or structure for the rest of your ideas.** Whether we admit it or not we all choose a *worldview* or a ***personal intellectual operating software.*** Some folks make a conscious choice, many people make it subconsciously or by default. The important thing to realize is that your worldview greatly affects ALL the other choices you make. In the computer world if you want to do graphics, you choose the Mac/Apple format, however; if you are just interested in word processing, Windows on a PC format may be better for you. There are other technology tasks where Linux might be the best operating system to use. If you are in business the SAP format may work best. From a personal spiritual perspective, choosing your *personal intellectual operating system* or your worldview is important just like choosing a computer operating system. Just like choosing operating software, the better you understand your "worldview" the better it will serve you in making decisions and organizing all the information we must deal with on a day-to-day basis for the rest of our life.

Another example is that your worldview is like the hidden formulas on an excel spreadsheet. Your outer life is the spreadsheet, but your worldview provides the formulas in the background that help give you the answers. It is your worldview in the background that does calculations that help you figure out answers about which actions to take.

Many people have differing thoughts on worldviews but for the purposes of this book we will use the definition that says your worldview must address four issues:

Origin - How did the world begin?

Meaning - What gives meaning to your existence?

Morality - What makes a thought or an action good or bad?

Future - What gives us hope or other expectations for the future?

A change in Worldviews or the Intellectual Gestalt shift

Now we will give an example of how a Worldview can change. It would be like "your spiritual operating system" going from a Windows based PC to a Mac based operating system.

Most people have taken a visual association test at some point in their lives. You are shown a vague drawing and you are asked "what do you see in this picture?" One such optical illusion or Gestalt shift looks to be an hourglass at first. But if you are told to look for it, you can see two silhouettes looking at each other instead.

The shift from seeing the same picture from one way to seeing it in another way is called a Gestalt shift or Gestalt switch. The important point here is that **the Gestalt shift**

can happen intellectually as well as visually. The worldview you approach the picture with can determine what you see. Whether it is a visual picture or an intellectual picture, once someone explains the other view you can see it as well. This is to say that to understand Spirituality sometimes you can begin to understand it by changing your worldview or changing your perspective.

Below is an example of a "Visual" Gestalt shift or optical illusion. It is called Rubin's Vase.

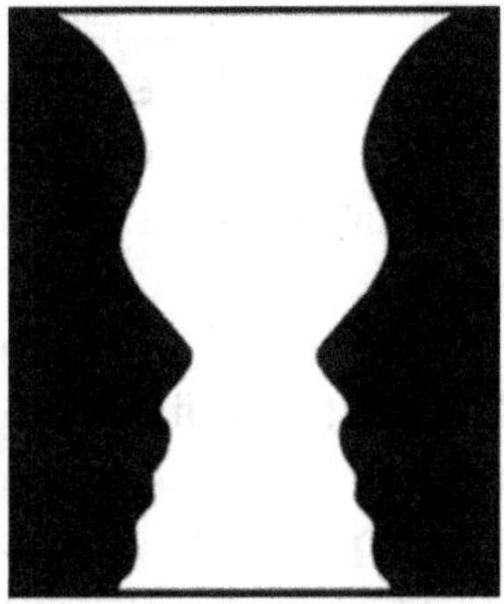

The above image is taken from:
https://commons.wikimedia.org/wiki/Category:Rubin%27s_vase

This drawing is an example of a visual Gestalt shift. In the drawing, if someone says, "do you see a white vase in the middle of a black background" you probably will see it. However, if they say "do you see two silhouettes staring at each other" you can probably blink and see that also.

Just as there are Visual or optical Gestalt shifts, there are also **intellectual or mental Gestalt shifts!**

The point here is to highlight the fact that the worldview you bring to your understanding of reality can help determine what you "see" or know, or how you understand or perceive things. Depending on how someone describes a situation or drawing you can see it either way, **so what you look for is what you will see.**

Here is another way to understand this shift of worldviews or an intellectual Gestalt Shift. It's like playing soccer by football rules. If you grew up in the USA and you saw a lot of American football but no soccer, then you went to England and people asked you if you wanted to play football, it is likely that when you first see the European football field you would run out with the team and you would start tackling and blocking and touching the ball with your hands. When the game starts you would get penalties because you don't understand how the game is played. You would say "well you asked me to play football". The problem is, what the English call football, Americans call soccer.

Even though the field looked a lot like American football, and even though they called it football, until you know the rules of the game, there is no way you can win or even be an effective player. You thought you were playing by the right rules, but you weren't. There was no way you could win or even compete effectively, and you would be confused and very stressed out and you would probably want to quit playing until you learned the rules.

To understand spirituality, or the spiritual world, you have to understand that there are spiritual laws just like there are physical laws, and **there are things you can do in the physical world that affect you in the spiritual world and vice versa.** If you are never taught the spiritual laws, you will never see the whole picture.

In the picture of the "vase" above. Someone who says they see a vase and no faces would be like someone saying there are no real spiritual laws in the real world, so they do not see reality in terms of a spiritual side. The goal of this book is to say **if you look for spiritual laws and spiritual effects in the natural or real world, you will see them**, just like if you look for two faces instead of a vase you will see them. Many times, you will not see the faces until someone points it out. **There are many patterns that exist in life that we do not see until someone points them out.**

To help someone move from a non-spiritual to a spiritual worldview or from a Secular to a Christian worldview, you need to help them make the "intellectual Gestalt shift" to take you from a worldview that only includes the physical laws to a worldview that also acknowledges spiritual laws. Many people are playing *the game of life* by the wrong rules. They are trying to play European football with American football rules.

Understanding today's culture
In the highly sexed, highly material world we live in today it can be hard to make the shift from seeing just the physical world to understanding the spiritual side of reality. All forms of media are financed by selling physical products, so we are constantly bombarded by products from the *material world.* Current culture is dominated by media advertisers that are trying to get you to look *beautiful,* which is defined as; thinner, sexier, and richer. The modern hip hop influenced culture is all about bling. Bling is the ultimate sign of material success. It is all about the physical, the way you move your body in dance or the amount of expensive jewelry, or gold chains, or tattoos you wear. You are judged by what you accumulate and acquire. Success is all about the physical material world. Meanwhile the education system is dominated by people who confuse religion with spirituality, and they are afraid of religion so they will not mention anything that has to do with the spiritual world. For the most part, the educational system is at the point where the spiritual world cannot be mentioned for fear of offending the less than 10% of people who do not believe in some form of spirituality.

To truly understand the spiritual world, you must learn, and understand, spiritual laws, spiritual acts, and spiritual consequences, just like you have learned to live by the physical laws. For those who are Christians you understand how God's laws or spiritual laws work. The way to help secular folks understand spiritual laws is to start by explaining the difference between physical and spiritual laws.

The more you understand about the spiritual laws, or the spiritual dimension to reality, the better you will understand the physical world, and the truer joy, and peace, you will experience in the physical world, because finally you understand more of the rules, and you can *enjoy playing the game*. The stress of not knowing what to expect or when you will be penalized is taken away. **To activate your spirit, or to get to the third stage of spiritual development, you must understand or at least acknowledge there is a spiritual side to reality.**

I contend the best way to get a non-believer to understand Christianity you first must help them understand there is a spiritual dimension to reality. Many people believe in a spiritual dimension of some sort, but they have not taken the time to really think about it and understand it. They have witnessed Christians who are hypocritical in one way or another, so they shy away from the Christian message because one or more people they know tried and failed to follow it. We are all weak, sinful people, so not being able to follow the message doesn't make the message bad or wrong, it shows how hard it is to lead a good life. Having a worldview that is consistent with the true order of reality helps us handle struggles and the many difficulties of everyday life.

Chapter 10 Study Questions

What is a worldview?

What are the four issues a worldview must address?

What is a Gestalt shift?

Do you understand the similarities of an optical Gestalt shift, or optical illusion and an intellectual gestalt shift?

How does the idea of playing soccer by football rules apply to living with a non- spiritual worldview?

What are some reasons why people choose a non-spiritual worldview?

What are some reasons to believe in a spiritual worldview?

Do you believe there are two sides to reality, a spiritual and a physical side? Why?

Chapter 11
Politics and Spirituality

Just like individual development, human social development goes through three stages:

- Primal / Tribal / Instinctual / Traditional cultures
- Cultures based on ideologies and reason
-         (Like Democracies or communism)
- Spiritual or God inspired cultures

Primal tribal cultures

Primal culture begins when primal humans walk out of their cave. They are motivated by **fear of the omnipotent unknown.** It is a time of intense negativity. They are constantly trying to understand and predict all the dangers that could happen to cause them harm. Individuals are motivated by self-preservation of themselves and their immediate family. Primal humans begin in family-based tribes that are ruled by force and the survival of the strongest person. Their mentality is an eye for an eye. The tribe is led by the strongest member.

Cultures Based on Reason and Consensus

In the course of human history, it was not until very recently that societies began to be organized by ideology, reason, and consensus, instead of instinct, emotions, tradition, and force.

In the time of Socrates (400 to 300 BC), the Greek culture had a flash of enlightenment and they started to develop Philosophy, Psychology, Democracy and an appreciation for Art and Morality. When Rome conquered Greece in 282 BC, much of the appreciation for the intellectual pursuits was lost or given less prominence.

The term Politics was first popularized by the Greeks. The Greek word Polis is translated as city, so politics is the affairs of the city, or society, or community. The Greek translation of community is, Com = with, uni = one. The goal of the community is to work with one, or as one. Those who run the city are usually called politicians and they decide the laws of justice, and how to distribute the common resources of the community.

There are two kinds of politicians. Those who are truly concerned about doing what is right for the common good, and those who are using their status as community representatives to increase their own wealth and influence.

Moses was the first human who tried to organize a society based on the laws of God or spiritual laws and not the laws of men. He was trying to make all the decisions by himself, and he was getting burned out. In Exodus 18:18 Moses's father-in-law Jethro told him, "The work is too heavy for you; you cannot handle it alone. Listen now to me and I will give you some advice, and may God be with your instructions. You must be the people's representative before God and bring their disputes to him. Teach them his decrees and show them the way they are to live and how they are to behave. [21] **But select capable men from all the people—men who fear God, trustworthy men who hate dishonest gain**—and appoint them as officials over thousands, hundreds, fifties and tens.

The term dishonest gain can be translated as corruption. Jethro gave Moses the **advice to delegate authority and to choose people who fear or respect God and hate corruption**. Because we live in such a populous, complex society the only way to exist is through a system of delegated authority. No matter how well the system is devised, when most of the people in authority are using the system for personal gain the system breaks down. The founders of the United States of America were brilliant, God inspired people. They studied every form of government from the Greeks to the Romans to the Monarchs of Europe. They realized that power corrupts, and absolute power corrupts absolutely. Their whole goal was to divide the power and create a system of checks and balances to keep a powerful corrupt group of people from taking control. The three branches of the U.S. government are designed after the three forms of government that had existed up until that time. The Executive branch was modeled after the Monarchs of Europe. The Senate was modeled after the Aristocracies. The congress was modeled after the relatively new idea of democracy or government by the consent of the governed. **The founders knew that ultimately, success would be based on the spiritual development of the people.**

Although the founders did everything they could to divide power between the states and the federal government. They knew no structure could survive unbridled greed. John Adams said, "We have no government armed with power capable of contending with human passions unbridled by morality and religion …. Our Constitution was made only for moral and religious people. It is wholly inadequate for the government by any other."[1]

Throughout human history, tyrannical leaders have hated God-worshippers because if people worshipped God, they were harder to control. To this day, there are many powerful politicians throughout the world that want individuals to depend on the government for their sense of dignity and even their income instead of depending on their God and their family.

For most of human history, other than brief periods for Israel, until the late 1700's societies were ruled by Monarchs, Emperors or Pharaohs. Most rulers believed in the philosophy of an *eye for an eye*, and *the strongest man wins*. I will refer to this as stage one social organization.

In ancient cultures it was thought that if you worshipped the wrong gods, you would make the gods mad, and it would bring bad things to the community. Nero persecuted Christians because he believed the bad things happening to him were because he allowed the Christians in the Empire to worship the wrong gods.

In medieval times the European Monarchs cleverly devised the *Divine Right of Kings* theory to help their absolute claim to power. The encyclopedia Britannica describes the theory as follows, "in European history, a political doctrine in defense of monarchical absolutism, which asserted that kings derived their authority from God and could not therefore be held accountable for their actions by any earthly authority such as a parliament. Originating in Europe, the divine-right theory can be traced to the medieval conception of God's award of temporal power to the political ruler, paralleling the award of spiritual power to the church. By the 16th and 17th centuries, however, the new national monarchs were asserting their authority in matters of both church and state. King James I of England (reigned 1603–25) was the foremost exponent of the divine right of kings."[2]

It is quite an irony that the foremost advocate of the Divine right of Kings was King James I who was the first to translate the Bible into English shortly after the invention of the printing press. It was the ability of the average person to understand the Bible themselves that caused individuals to question what the Priests were teaching them. The newfound understanding of the Bible caused the Puritans and Pilgrims in England to want more religious freedom.
Under the religious leadership of William Brewster, John Robinson, William Bradford and others, the Christian separatists fled from England to Amsterdam, then Leiden, Holland to escape persecution by King James. Bradford and the Pilgrims were imprisoned more than once for their religious beliefs, and they eventually fled to America on the Mayflower and started the Plymouth Colony in Massachusetts.

Separation of Church and State

Jesus was the first major figure in history to acknowledge the separation of church and state when he said, "Give to Caesar what is Caesar's and to God what is God's."[3] Most communities have struggled to figure out how to bring about the blessings of God into a corporate social structure.

Nowhere in the founding documents of the USA will you find anything about separating God from politics. The term separation of powers was used in a letter by Thomas Jefferson to keep the Government from trying to interfere with religion. The reason many people left England was because the **English Government controlled the Anglican Church**. The intent was not to take God out of government **but to keep the Government from controlling the church**.

"The two 'religion clauses' of the First Amendment appear at the beginning of the Amendment *'Congress shall make no law respecting an establishment of religion'* (the Establishment Clause) *'or prohibiting the free exercise thereof* '(The Free Exercise Clause). As constitutional scholar George Goldberg stated, 'it was equally agreed that, just as the Federal government should be prohibited from telling people how to worship, it should be prohibited from telling them how not to worship."[4]

The Moses Dilemma

Ultimately, if you believe the third stage of human development is the spiritual stage, then it brings us back to the Moses dilemma. How to organize a society based on the laws of God and spiritual laws not the laws of humans. That is a subject for another book, but finding people who are truly interested in doing what is right for the common good and not trying to make themselves rich by swaying to influence is the key. Finding political leaders who are motivated by the sacrificial love for others like Jesus, seems to be a very, very, difficult task, but that should be our goal.

Chapter 11 Study Questions

What are the three stages of social development?

What is politics?

What advice did Jethro give to Moses about who should help him rule society?

Who was the first major human figure to discuss Separation of Church and State?

How would you suggest we find leaders who would put the good of the community above their own personal gain?

Chapter 12
The Way Forward
Spiritual Life and Spiritual Death

We have talked about the Paradox of Human Existence, which is that humans have a spiritual nature, but we realize and actualize our spiritual nature through a physical body. Your Spiritual Life begins when you realize and begin to explore your spiritual nature. Until you realize your spiritual nature, and that there is a spiritual dimension to reality, regardless of your religion or spiritual worldview, you are physically alive but spiritually dead.

We talked about Existentialism and the idea there is no spiritual dimension to reality. We mentioned if all you believe in is time, matter, and chance, your life is about obtaining more pleasure than pain, and nothing else.

We talked about worldviews, and how everyone must decide what their worldview is because your worldview is the structure for your thoughts, much like an operating system is for a computer. Your worldview must supply a structure for understanding meaning and morality and your goals for the future.

My secular translation of the Christian Gospel is that since the beginning of time God has been trying to help humans understand their spiritual nature. It was a long, slow process. When human beings were at the point they developed a sense of a personal ego and their own free will (Adam and Eve), they separated themselves from God's Will, which means they lost the true sense of spiritually (they died spiritually). Human history since that time has been about humans rediscovering their sense of spirituality and understanding their spiritual nature. Christians call this, God trying to bring a fallen, or sinful people, back unto Himself. **The secular translation of the true meaning of the life of Jesus is** that He was the first moral philosopher to discuss how to put spiritual laws into physical practice. He was the first human to discuss spirituality, the true nature of a single Creator personal God, and our personal relation to that God. Christians know Jesus is much more that that but that is a great first step.

The Hebrews before Jesus struggled to live by the laws God gave them. Jesus *raised the bar* and explained who God was and why we should follow those rules. Forgiveness, Grace, sacrificial love, treating all humans as fully human, loving people from other cultures are all concepts that Jesus initiated and clarified for ALL of humanity. Jesus was the first human rights advocate. Everything Jesus said and did was so far outside the norm of anything anyone had ever thought about before that time that if it was a made-up story, it had to be created by someone who was intellectually and spiritually prophetic, and well advanced of anyone else at that time. I tell people who deny the many historical accounts of Jesus that if Jesus did not live and do the things the Bible describes, whoever made up the story should be called a Messianic prophet. It is a historical fact that the people who wrote the New Testament were friends and followers of Jesus. **The words and actions of Jesus truly were the Messianic message that ushered in the age of spirituality for mankind.**

Jesus was the human form of God, because God had to step into humanity and help humans realize there is a spiritual dimension to reality, and we can have a relationship with a personal God who loves us like a perfect Father loves his children. For those who do not have a father, or they have a bad father, it is difficult to understand. I have tried to point out that in ancient times it was extremely difficult for humans to understand the concept of a personal Creator God. **It is still difficult today.** The concept of spirituality is almost impossible for the physical mind to understand because it is beyond reason and logic. Without God showing up in human physical form, and being resurrected, there is no telling if the human mind would have ever developed the concept of spirituality.

108

Christians believe that to wake humans up about their spiritual nature and to show His love for His *children*, God realized He would have to come to earth in human form and perform many kinds of ***supernatural acts* of Divine Love**. God's goal has always been to help humans realize **that spiritual life is more important than, and the ultimate goal of, physical life**. Jesus healed the sick, the blind, the deaf, and the mentally handicapped. He treated men, women, children, and people of other cultures as equals, as fully human, because they were ALL created in God's Image and worthy of dignity. One of God's many goals was to free the spiritually oppressed. Jesus suffered every abuse known to humankind. He was beaten, mocked, whipped, paraded through the streets carrying the cross he would die on, and hung on that cross naked (which was sexual abuse) in front of his family and friends.

Jesus was totally sinless and innocent. The mob, the Roman rulers, and those who betrayed him exhibit the sins that we all embody. His presence represented the right way to live, and it was such a contrast to the corrupt political and religious power structure of the time, they twisted HIs words and actions to find an excuse to have him killed. Unfortunately, not much has changed in two-thousand years. When you try to help people become spiritually free, there will be many who oppose you.

Jesus's words and actions demonstrated the perfect representation of the ***Way*** to live. His words were the ***Truth*** of Life. He died to prove that your Spirit outlives your body, and every human being has the capacity for ***Spiritual Life*** after death.

The greatest human fear is the fear of death. Jesus faced that fear and conquered the fear of death for all people forever.

Like everything else in life, you will not see a pattern unless you look for it. There are patterns all around us. Much of what science does is discover the physical patterns of life, but you don't know they are there unless you look for them or someone teaches you about them. It took humans many millennia to realize the pattern of planetary rotation and that the earth rotated around the sun. You will not see God's pattern unless you look for it.

Medicine doesn't work unless you ingest it. Unless you allow Jesus's Spirit to become part of you, the medicine that has been revealed does you no good. The more you learn about God's pattern in the Universe, the more comfortable you will be dealing with the many difficult circumstances of the physical life.

God sent His Son as proof positive that if we search for and believe in God, we will have a relationship with Him. Like any other relationship, it may take time for you to develop a trust in the other person which starts with believing in the other person. The reason many people deny the spiritual dimension to reality, or God's world, is because they have a false sense that freedom is being able to do whatever you want, whenever you want to. **The Truth is that there is a Divine Order to all things and true freedom is realizing that order and living within that structure. All freedom is freedom within limits.**

We talked about the relationship between the individual and the larger social group. We understand church and state must be separate. Nations based on the Laws and Will of God will certainly outlast nations based on the laws of men. We should not have Christian nations; we should have nations of Christians.

Jesus's whole message was about changing people's hearts (spirits). Unless people have good strong spirits and character, no system can be devised to protect society from self-destruction. The optimistic news is the reverse is also true. No matter how bad the system of government is, if the people's spirits are in the right place, society can survive and flourish. The key is to get the order of a society in sync with God's order.

There are many more deep things we could say to unpack the true depth of the Christian Gospel, but I will leave it here for now.

I will close by saying all life comes down to the dilemma Adam and Eve faced. **Are you self-centered or are you God-centered?** Are your actions for yourself and your community self-centered or God Centered? Are you trying your best to represent (re-present) the life of Jesus or are you just concerned about expressing your own personal will and ego? Whether or not you believe Jesus was the Son of God or the Messiah, you cannot find a better role model and you cannot find a human being who did a better job of speaking and acting in accordance with God's Will. Jesus is the standard for human moral thought and action.

Life is difficult. Realizing and actualizing your spiritual nature is difficult. Many people think it is difficult to have a relationship with God. It gets easier the more you understand it. Having a relationship with The Creator starts whenever you decide to start it.

We have traced the history of the Spiritual development of Human History. We see the progress from primal/ tribal/ emotional /traditional, motivations for actions, to ideological or reason based, and then to being spiritual, or God based motivations for words and actions. The Christian calls this believing in your heart (spirit) and speaking with your mouth that Jesus is your Savior.

Some Humans are just beginning to realize their spiritual nature. We are all involved in a two-step process: **realizing, then actualizing, our spiritual nature**. You can begin by changing your words, then your actions, and then you must work to help structure our social institutions in a manner that augments the spiritual nature of humans. God works through humans, so unless Godly people get involved and change the institutions, the institutions will be generally sinful and oppressive. If you do not oppose evil, you get more of it.

The question to keep asking yourself is this, is this word, this action, or the goal of this institution to help me or a small group of individuals, or to help others and society as a whole?

We are so highly interdependent that your words and actions, whether they are good or bad, cannot help but affect and be noticed by others.

Something within us yearns for that which transcends the physical. It yearns for truth, wholeness, and unity. When we feel the Presence of God, we not only get beyond ourselves, but we also enter the spiritual dimension of which we all are a part.

The paradox of human existence is that the hard part of (physical) life is learning to die to all the material temptations of the physical life and learning to live for The Spiritual Life.

Be God centered, not self-centered.

THE END

The author's prayer for his readers:

Ephesians 1:13 When you believed, you were marked in him with a seal, the promised Holy Spirit, I keep asking that the God of our Lord Jesus Christ, the glorious Father, may give you the Spirit of wisdom and revelation, so that you may know him better.

I pray that the eyes of your heart may be enlightened in order that you may know the hope to which He has called you, the riches of his glorious inheritance in his holy people.

Study Questions and Answers

Introduction

Why is it good to understand how to describe Christianity in secular terms?
> Christianity is a very complex spiritual worldview. Learning to describe it in secular language makes it easier for most people to understand.

What is the Great Paradox of Human Existence?
> The fact that we are spiritual in nature, but we come to the realization of our spiritual nature through a physical body.

What is the 'Nature of Education'?
> Comparing what you know to something new you do not know.

Do you believe there are spiritual laws just like there are physical laws?
> Personal Answer

What is Presentism? Judging the past by present terms.

Chapter 1

How does a baby begin to process information?
> By comparing itself to other things.

What does it mean to be a 'Self-aware I'?
> You realize you have free will.
> You realize you can begin to control your destiny.

What are two ways the spiritual world manifests itself into the physical world?
> Through your words and actions.

Describe the difference between natural/instinctual, rational, and spiritual motivations for actions?
> Hoarding food for yourself and others is a natural **Instinct**.
> Sharing with someone who can pay you back is a **rational** or intellectual thought.
> Giving to others because they need help is **spiritual**.

What does it mean to be spiritually 'self-aware'?
> You are aware of your spiritual nature.

What is meant by Faith is like a magnifying glass?
> You can turn God's energy that you cannot see into words and actions that you can see.

What is meant by your Love is like a prism?
> God's light shines through you and shows beautiful colors through your words and actions.

Does it make sense to say a created being can understand the Creator?
> A created being cannot understand the true nature and complexities of The Creator.

What is meant by God's DNA?
>The part of God's spirit that is within all of us.

How is getting to know God like getting to know a friend?
>The more time you spend with God the better you get to know God.

What does it mean to be *married to God*?
>You have an intimate relationship with God. You consider God in everything you do.

Do you believe The Spirit of God can dwell in you?
>Only you can answer that question.

Chapter 2

Are humans independent or Interdependent?
>The more history progresses, the more interdependent we have become.

What are the three stages of individual development?
>Physical Body.
>Intellectual/ Mind/ Reason/ Psyche.
>Spiritual.

What are the three stages of social development?
>Primal/ tribal/ instinctual/ emotional / traditional
>Ideological/ rational
>Spiritual

When did many countries begin to transition from Monarchies to democracies?
>Late 1700's and 1800s.

When did a nation other than Israel become spiritually organized?
>Stay tuned.

Chapter 3

What four things must a Spiritual Worldview explain?
　　Origin
　　Morality
　　Meaning
　　Future

What were the early gods like?
　　All kinds of things. Some were animals, some were
　　part animal, part human, some were all human.
　　They were projections of people's imagination and
　　fears.

Why was Abraham "Chosen"?
　　He was the only person that listened and responded
　　to God.

What was the first thing God told Abraham to do?
　　Leave his home, his country, his culture and
　　his traditions.

Why does the author say Abraham was the father of social
Spiritual Consciousness?
　　He was the first person of that age who structured
　　his family based on God's spiritual laws or
　　instructions and not instincts, emotions, and
　　traditions.

How does Genesis describe Sin?
　　Separating yourself from God's Will.
　　Being self-centered NOT God-centered.

Does God honor your Free Will if you choose to do evil?
　　He honors your Free Will more than He desires a
　　sinless world.

Was Abraham the only person that God tried to speak to?
　　This is a good question to think about–God Knows

Chapter 4

What does it mean to be created in the image of God?
> God is a spirit. An image is a representation. Humans are spirits that have the potential to represent God in a physical form.

What does it mean when John said "In the beginning was the Word, and the Word was God, and the Word was with God?
> Words are one way the spiritual word manifests itself into the physical world. Jesus is the physical manifestation of God. Jesus is the third person of the Godhead, so Jesus was with God and He was God.

> (See chapter 6 for a better explanation of the Godhead or Trinity)

Chapter 5

Was there a general concept of forgiveness before Jesus?
No.

What was the name of the Hebrew tradition that cast out a family member who associated with people from other cultures?
Kezazah.

What is the name of the parable where Jesus first began to radically change the human concept of forgiveness?
The Prodigal Son.

What story talks about Jesus's thoughts about Women's Rights?
The story of Jesus visiting Martha and Mary, Lazarus' sisters.

In what parable did Jesus talk about loving your enemy and caring for people of other cultures?
The Good Samaritan.

What story talked about Jesus forgiving a woman caught in adultery?
Stoning the woman caught in adultery.

Chapter 6

Name two prophets who talked about the Holy Spirit?
> Jeremiah and Isaiah prophesied about it.

What is the significance of Adam and Eve eating the forbidden fruit?
> What you eat becomes part of you and can have eternal or generational consequences.
> If you separate yourself from God's Will, it has eternal negative consequences.

Does God violate our Free Will?
> No, he values your free will more than He values a sinless world.

What is the author's definition of Sin? (capital S)
> Separation from God. The more you separate yourself from God, the more sins (small s) you will commit.

What action changed the debate about spirituality and the afterlife?
> The Resurrection of Jesus.

Was The New Covenant about Laws?
> No, it was about loving God and doing His Will because you love God, and you have a
> relationship with Him, not because you are afraid of Him.
> It is about understanding your spirit not just your emotion or intellect or reason.

Chapter 7

What are the three stages of human social development?
    Primal/tribal
    Intellectual/Reason
    Spiritual

What Roman Emperor ended the persecution of Christians?
    Constantine.

What was the first attempt to standardize the Christian Religion?
    Council of Nicaea.

What was one of the main complaints of Martin Luther's 97 treatises that helped start the Reformation?
    You are saved by God's Grace, not by paying penances to the church. You are saved by Faith, not works.

Chapter 8

What drove Christopher Columbus to believe he would find a new world West of Europe?
    A calling from the Holy Spirit.

What was unique about the Mayflower Compact?
    It was the first time a group of free individuals created a government based on a social contract that was created by the consent of the governed and witnessed by God.

Why did the phrase *endowed by their creator with certain inalienable rights* have to come from the Biblical worldview?
    No other religion or ideology believed in humans were created in the image of a personal Creator God.

Chapter 9

Do you, or does anyone you know, have a worldview that says everything is just a result of time, matter, and chance?

Personal answer

What were the basic principles of Christian thought in the 1600's?

There is a personal Creator God.

Knowledge is revealed through scripture and prayer.

God appeared to humanity in the form of Jesus.

Morality is based on Scripture or the Word of God.

What ideas changed when Science and Reason replaced the Christian Worldview?

All history becomes the history of physical things.

What you believe is irrelevant if you cannot touch it, or test it.

Knowledge of the world comes through human reason or science, not through scripture or prayer.

Morality is based on individual reason, not on scripture or something objective and transcendent.

What are some of the key ideas of Naturalism?

Man does not learn through reason. Man observes Nature. Nature is all there is.

There is no spiritual or transcendent reality.

Man's cognitive ability separates him from animals, there is nothing fundamentally different.

What ideas changed to move people from Naturalism to Existentialism?

> Nihilism negates everything. It negates all purpose, all value, all meaning.

What are some of the consequences of Existential thought?

> Nothing has meaning. You do what feels good to you. You are not worried about right or wrong.

Can you have a moral law based on Existentialism?

> No, everyone is doing their own thing. Your only goal in life is to increase your pleasure and avoid pain.

Give historical examples of what happens when political leaders adopt an existential worldview.

> The strongest man rules. There is no right or wrong.

> The most powerful rule the weak

> All actions can be self-justified. Mass murder is just a part of controlling the masses.

Chapter 10

What is a worldview?

> Intellectual structure that helps you organize your thoughts and actions. It is like a computer operating system.

What are the four issues a worldview must address?

> Origin, Meaning, Morality, Future.

What is a Gestalt shift?

> An optical illusion. A picture where you can see two different images from the same picture.

Do you understand the similarities of an optical Gestalt shift, or optical illusion and an intellectual gestalt shift?

> An intellectual Gestalt Shift is when two people can think about the same event or idea in two different ways depending on their perspective.

How does the idea of playing soccer by football rules apply to living with a non- spiritual worldview?

> If you don't understand the rules of the game, you cannot win, and you will be frustrated and confused.

What are some reasons why people choose a non-spiritual worldview?

> Something bad has happened to them. They don't want to subject themselves to the discipline of rules that God wants us to live by.

What are some reasons to believe in a spiritual worldview?

> The fact that the world could be created by chance does not make sense to you. You have witnessed a miracle. One or more unexplainable circumstances have happened to you, and you know that they could not have happened by chance. You have felt God's presence in your life.

Do you believe there are two sides to reality, a spiritual and a physical side? Why?

Personal answer.

Chapter 11

What are the three stages of social development?

- Primal / Tribal / Instinctual / Traditional. Cultures based or Nations based on "survival of the fittest", and the strongest rule.
- Cultures based on ideologies, reason and consensus.   (Like Democracies or communism)
- Spiritual, or God inspired cultures or nations.

What is politics?

The early Greeks believed "politics" was managing the affairs of the city, and   deciding how to create laws of justice, and how to distribute the common resources of the community.

What advice did Jethro give to Moses about who should help him rule society?

Jethro told Moses, he should find capable people who fear God, and hate corruption.

Who was the first major human figure to discuss separation of Church and State?

Jesus, when He said, "give back to Caesar what is Caesar's, and to God what is God's". Mark 12:17

How would you suggest we find leaders who would put the good of the community above their own personal gain?

That is a difficult question. Each person must decide for themselves.

Footnotes

Chapter 1

1. Guillen, Michael. *Believing Is Seeing: A Physicist Explains How Science Shattered His Atheism and Revealed the Necessity of Faith*. (Tyndale House Publishers). (p. i). Kindle Edition. Pg. 7.

2. *ibid.*, Pg 26.

Chapter 2

1. video The children of Socrates Socrates' Children: An Introduction to Philosophy from the 100 Greatest Philosophers (wordonfire.org) https://books.wordonfire.org/socrateschildren

Chapter 3

1. Hamilton, Edith. *Mythology* (75th Anniversary Illustrated Edition) (BLACK DOG & LEV) . Running Press. Kindle Edition. Pg 29.

Chapter 4

None

Chapter 5

1. Ortberg, John, *Who Is This Man*, (Zondervan 2012), book pg.174.

2. *Ibid.*, p.176.

3. *Ibid.*, p.179.

4. Kezazah definition https://www.biola.edu/blogs/biola-magazine/2010/the-prodigal-sons-father-shouldnt-have-run

Chapter 6

1. Guillen, *Believing Is Seeing:* p.49.

2. Genesis 2:17.

3. Matthew 5:29.

Chapter 7

1. Holland, Tom. *Dominion* (pp. 13-14). Basic Books. Kindle Edition. P7.

2. https://en.wikipedia.org/wiki/Appointment_of_Catholic_bishops

3. https://en.wikipedia.org/wiki/Constantine_the_Great

4. https://classroom.synonym.com/caused-england-catholic-church-separate-6935.html

Chapter 8

1. Marshall, Peter J.; Manuel, David B. *The Light and the Glory* (God's Plan for America Book #1): 1492-1793 (p. 14). Baker Publishing Group. Kindle Edition.

2. https://www.history.com/topics/colonial-america/jamestown

3. Limbaugh, David, *Persecution, How Liberals are Waging War Against Christianity,* (Washington, D.C., Regnery Publishing, Inc. 2003), p.302.

4. *ibid.*, p.303.

5. *ibid.*, p.302.

6. Marshall, *The Light and the Glory,* p.182.

7. Marshall, *The Light and the Glory,* p.236.

8. Limbaugh, *Persecution*, p. 311.

9. *ibid.,* 308.

10. *ibid.*, p.309.

Chapter 9

1. Sire, James W., *The Universe Next Door,* (Intervarsity Press Downers Grove IL. 1997), p.23-38.

2. *ibid.,* p.43.

3. *ibid.,* p.46.

4. *ibid.,* p.71.

5. *ibid.,* p.73.

6. Johnson, Paul, *Intellectuals,* (New York: Harper & Row, 1988), p.246.

7. Shirer, William, *The Rise and Fall of The Third Reich: A History of Nazi Germany* (New York: Simon and Shuster, 1960), p.100.

8. Hitler, Adolf, in Norman Geisler, "Wretched Refuse," Kindred Spirit, August 1988.

9. Zacharias, Ravi, *The End of Reason* (Zondervan, Grand Rapids, MI. 2008), ebook p.58.

10. *ibid.,* p.60.

11.https://www.goodreads.com/author/show/1938.Friedrich _Nietzsche

12. Guillen, *Believing Is Seeing:* p.185.

Chapter 10

None

Chapter 11

1. Evans, Stanton, The Theme in Freedom, Religion, politics, and the American Tradition, (Washington, D.C.: Regnery Publishing, Inc. 1994). P.317.

2. https://www.britannica.com/topic/divine-right-of-kings

3. Matthew 22:21.

4. Persecution pg. 322.

Chapter 12

None

Bibliography

Definition https://www.biola.edu/blogs/biola-magazine/2010/the-prodigal-sons-father-shouldnt-have-run Kezazah definition

https://www.britannica.com/topic/divine-right-of-kings

https://classroom.synonym.com/caused-england-catholic-church-separate-6935.html

Evans, Stanton, The Theme in Freedom, Religion, politics and the American Tradition, (Washington, D.C.: Regnery Publishing, Inc. 1994).

https://www.goodreads.com/author/show/1938.Friedrich_Nietzsche

Guillen, Michael. *Believing Is Seeing: A Physicist Explains How Science Shattered His Atheism and Revealed the Necessity of Faith.* (Tyndale House Publishers). (p. i). Kindle Edition. Pg.

Hamilton, Edith. *Mythology* (75th Anniversary Illustrated Edition) (BLACK DOG & LEV). Running Press. Kindle Edition.

https://www.history.com/topics/colonial-america/jamestown

Hitler, Adolf, in Norman Geisler, "Wretched Refuse," Kindred Spirit, August 1988.

Holland, Tom. *Dominion* (pp. 13-14). Basic Books. Kindle Edition.

Johnson, Paul, *Intellectuals,* (New York: Harper & Row, 1988).

Limbaugh, David, *Persecution, How Liberals are Waging War Against Christianity,* (Washington, D.C., Regnery Publishing, Inc. 2003).

Marshall, Peter J.; Manuel, David B. *The Light and the Glory* (God's Plan for America Book #1): 1492-1793 Baker Publishing Group. Kindle Edition.

Ortberg, John, *Who Is This Man*, (Zondervan 2012), book pg.

Shirer, William, *The Rise and Fall of The Third Reich: A History of Nazi Germany* (New York: Simon and Shuster, 1960),

Sire, James W., *The Universe Next Door,* (Intervarsity Press Downers Grove IL. 1997),

https://en.wikipedia.org/wiki/Appointment_of_Catholic_bish ops

https://en.wikipedia.org/wiki/Constantine_the_Great

video The children of Socrates <u>Socrates' Children: An Introduction to Philosophy from the 100 Greatest Philosophers (wordonfire.org)</u> <u>https://books.wordonfire.org/socrateschildren</u>

Zacharias, Ravi, *The End of Reason* (Zondervan, Grand Rapids, MI. 2008), ebook

About the Author

Bob was born, raised, and resides in the Cincinnati, Ohio area. He graduated from Culver Military Academy High School in Culver, Indiana, and earned a Bachelor of Arts Degree from Miami University in Oxford, Ohio, where he majored in Philosophy and Political Science. Bob and his wife, Upasna, have been married for over thirty-five years. They raised two boys, both of whom are happily married. They have four grandchildren.

As a national sales manager in the wholesale hardware and commercial cleaning products industries, Bob has traveled extensively throughout North America during his career. Bob attends church regularly and is often a teacher or participant in Bible and book study classes. Bob's favorite pastimes are reading, biking, spending time with his family, and writing. Next to these, Bob finds joy helping charities whose mission is to create generational change for forgotten, abused, and orphaned children locally as well as in Kerala, India, and Kenya, Africa.

Bob's wife Upasna, or, "Pasna" as she is called in the U.S., was just 16 when she left India by herself, making her one of the youngest single people to ever get a visa to the USA at that time. Since getting married over thirty-five years ago, Bob and Pasna have traveled to India eight times, visiting the Taj Mahal on seven of those trips. On three of the trips, they took groups of friends and students to show them parts of the world they probably would never have seen otherwise. Their joy of traveling has also taken them to Europe, South America, and Dubai. Over the years, Bob and Pasna have hosted foreign students from Brazil, Norway, Thailand, India, Tajikistan, Spain, Lithuania, and Puerto Rico.

Bob is retired from his business career. He and Pasna spend their time with family and traveling to discuss his books. Bob's books and discussions are part of the mission Bob calls, *The Spiritual Puzzle Project*. Bob's mission is to help people understand their spiritual nature more fully and be comfortable sharing their beliefs with others.

Find more about The Spiritual Puzzle online at
Website www.thespiritualpuzzle.com

**Understanding the
Spiritual Puzzle**

www.thespiritualpuzzle.com

Facebook SpiritualPuzzle

Twitter@SpiritualPuzzle

Instagram@TheSpiritualPuzzle